CONCILIUM

THEOLOGY IN THE AGE OF RENEWAL

CONCILIUM

CONCILIUM/VOL. 23

PASTORAL THEOLOGY

THE PASTORAL
APPROACH TO
ATHEISM

edited by KARL RAHNER, S.J.

VOLUME 23

CONCILIUM
theology in the age of renewal

PAULIST PRESS
NEW YORK, N.Y. / GLEN ROCK, N.J.

PAULIST PRESS
EXECUTIVE OFFICES: 304 W. 58th Street, New York, N.Y. and 21 Harristown Road, Glen Rock, N.J.
Executive Publisher: John A. Carr, C.S.P.
Executive Manager: Alvin A. Illig, C.S.P.
Asst. Executive Manager: Thomas E. Comber, C.S.P.

EDITORIAL OFFICES: 304 W. 58th Street, New York, N.Y.
Editor: Kevin A. Lynch, C.S.P.
Managing Editor: Urban P. Intondi

Printed and bound in the United States of America by
The Colonial Press Inc., Clinton, Mass.

CONTENTS

PART II

BIBLIOGRAPHICAL SURVEY

PART III

DO-C DOCUMENTATION CONCILIUM

Preface

Karl Rahner, S.J./*Munich, West Germany*

No question is more important and topical for the Church today than the question of how to approach the problem of atheism spiritually and pastorally. Vatican Council II did indeed touch upon it, but only on the periphery of the dominant theme of the Council. Therefore, post-conciliar theology is in danger of becoming introverted, concentrating on explicit conciliar themes such as liturgy, ecclesiology, ecumenism and canon law in a way that underrates the decisive issue of atheism in its peculiar contemporary form and menace. All other questions yield in importance to this one. The Church must serve man according to the witness she gives of herself as formulated by the Council. She can only do this if she leads him to God and proclaims God's glory in a world which believes that God is no longer to be found and which talks glibly about the "death of God".

The Church must witness to God, not merely among those who belong to her visibly because of a straightforward social and historical situation, nor only among those she may hope to win over by some direct means, but also, as far as possible, among all those who are neither Christians nor likely to become so in the foreseeable future. Therefore, all those who believe in God must join in this struggle. One should not reject such a common approach from the start on the ground that "God" does not mean the same thing in the various religions. If there is truth in the various conciliar statements, which maintain that grace and justification are also possible outside the Church and outside Christianity, then all those who confess God cannot be simply said to confess a different God in spite of whatever errors and confusion may mar their image of God. There is, therefore, a factual basis for a common witness to God in an atheistic world.

Concilium, Vol. 6, has already dealt with this question but this does not mean that we should not build further on the basic and general statements worked out there in the direction of pastoral theology. Nor will anyone who understands pastoral theology expect this work to be less laborious.

We need, first of all, an analysis of the conciliar texts that deal with atheism. This will imply questions that the Council has not solved. If the article that deals with this establishes that there is an "implicit" theism in modern atheism, this should not be interpreted as making an explicit theism superfluous or unimportant; rather, it points to that necessary and always present condition of any explicit witness and confession of God without which any approach to atheism is bound to be absolutely hopeless or exposed to totally false aims and methods.

Several articles deal with various aspects of this problem of how to approach atheism. The discussion of the basis for a theology of unbelief on the evidence of modern literature brings out the internal differences that obtain within this atheism. One should remember that the article on the psychological and sociological aspects of modern atheism does *not* deal with the metaphysical and theological question of God's existence, but with specifically psychological and sociological factors in theism and atheism.

The same warning to remember what is and what is not being talked about also holds for other articles. Anyone who has a truly "pastoral" awareness will welcome this open empirical approach. That these factors are not seen as isolated and autonomous is clear from the sketch of pastoral "maxims" required for preaching the faith to modern unbelievers. The modest attempt at establishing a "short formula of the faith" shows how much new thinking is required for the actual preaching of the faith.

The article on "religious indifference" brings out how difficult and almost futile any dialogue with unbelievers is and how carefully one must beware of fashionable presentations. The extensive bibliographical survey is meant to complement the survey of *Concilium,* Vol. 6, and shows the concrete and tactical onslaught on Christianity by a frankly militant atheism. This article provides much authentic material which is not easily accessible to the average reader. A priest who has had many contacts with "unbelievers" points to what is required for a truly personal encounter with an unbeliever, particularly in the case of a priest. The Secretary himself contributes a report on the Secretariat for Unbelievers to show how seriously the official Church takes this task of coming to grips with modern atheism.

This volume is obviously but a small contribution to an almost endless task and an immeasurable need. Insofar as the Editor and his collaborators are concerned this means not only that such work must be constantly subjected to severe criticism—and of this they are fully aware—but also that the attempt is ultimately justified. *In magnis voluisse sat est*—great enterprises must begin with the will to achieve.

PART I
ARTICLES

Karl Rahner, S.J./*Munich, West Germany*

What Does Vatican II Teach about Atheism?

Although Vatican Council II did not deal with atheism in a special decree, it was so much on the mind of the Council that it has to be reckoned as one of the real subjects of the Council's debates and decisions. This is not self-evident. The Council intended to be, and in fact became, a pastoral Council,[1] but this does not by itself explain why it should busy itself with atheism. The fact is that today the question of a socially accepted, worldwide atheism, which is also to some extent politically militant, has become so urgent that a "pastoral" Council could not possibly avoid it.

And yet, one cannot honestly say that the fact and problems of contemporary atheism loomed so large in the minds of the Council fathers that it had to be dealt with officially in the Church. The mentality of the fathers was not on the whole fully aware of the position of Christianity in a specifically atheistic age, as is shown by the following, perhaps not very striking, fact: there is no doubt that the various dogmatic and pastoral constitutions and decrees were major theological and pastoral achieve-

[1] To understand the pastoral element in the light of the Council and particularly with reference to the *Pastoral Constitution on the Church in the Modern World,* see K. Rahner, "Zur Theologischen Problematik einer 'Pastoralkonstitution'" (A contribution to a collection with commentaries on this Constitution, to be published by Paul Brand, Hilversum, and also to appear in various translations).

ments, but careful reading shows that on the whole (and particularly in the *Pastoral Constitution on the Church in the Modern World*) the conciliar fathers were not so directly concerned with the contemporary atheist that they would immediately attract his attention. Too often—for example, when it is said that God is the only solution for all human problems—the language used seems to take for granted that every man today, whether believer or unbeliever, should obviously understand what is meant by the term "God",[2] although the Pastoral Constitution itself declares that there are many people today to whom, in their own mind, religious language is wholly meaningless. Therefore, it is not self-evident that the Council concerned itself explicitly with atheism. Therefore, one is grateful to the Spirit for having steered this Council in such a way that, in fact, it *did* concern itself with atheism.

I

The Conciliar Texts on Atheism

The most important text on atheism occurs naturally in nn. 19-21 of the *Pastoral Constitution On the Church in the Modern World*. Other texts, however, should be added to this one, such as par. 5 of n. 22 of the same Constitution; a short text in n. 16 of the *Dogmatic Constitution On the Church*; n. 7 of the *Decree On the Missionary Activity of the Church*, which contains a statement about the potential faith of a man whom the Gospel message has not reached, a statement that is surely related to our theme; and, finally, there are the references in the *Decree On the Pastoral Office of Bishops in the Church* (nn. 11 and 13) and in the *Decree On the Ministry and Life of Priests* (n. 4) to preaching to unbelievers where this preaching, in a manner adapted to their situation, is counted among the most urgent duties of bishops and priests.[3]

[2] For this problem, see K. Rahner, "In Search of a Short Formula of the Christian Faith," in this volume of *Concilium*.

[3] This does not mean that all the significant texts of the Council are gathered here, but they show in which sense other texts should also be interpreted.

To give here an extensive commentary on nn. 19-21 of the *Pastoral Constitution on the Church in the Modern World* would exceed the framework of this small contribution.[4] Therefore, I hope it may suffice to indicate what is decidedly new in this text and then to draw some conclusions from this and to point out some problems.

II

What Is New in the Conciliar Texts?

I shall not attempt here an analysis of how each of these texts differs from the customary "Scholastic" theology (*Schultheologie*). For our present purpose there are, above all, two new and surprising developments in the teaching on atheism.

A New View of the Question of Moral Guilt in Positive Atheism

First of all, although the Council dealt somewhat extensively with atheism, it ignored the traditional Scholastic thesis which held that a normally intelligent man could not be a positive atheist over a more or less protracted period without moral guilt.[5] One can go beyond that and say that the Council did not merely lay this thesis aside but that it put forward an *opposite thesis,* namely, that it is possible for *a normal adult to accept an explicit atheism for a longer period,* even till the end of his life, *without any proof of moral guilt* on the part of the unbeliever. This thesis is not set out in so many words but is implied in the reference to the fact that, on the one hand, there exists an explicit atheism, which is widespread socially and held to be self-evident in all simplicity, while on the other hand, general Christian principles do not entitle us simply to condemn such atheists as being gravely

---

[4] Such a commentary should also contain a history of how the text of nn. 19-21 came about, with the many *vota* of the fathers that belong to it. But this is also too much to be attempted here.

[5] For the evidence and closer interpretation, see the dogmatic textbooks, e.g., Patres Societatis Jesu facultatum theol. in Hispania professores, *Sacra theologiae Summa* II (4th ed. Madrid, 1964), pp. 23-4, with notes 21 and 22.

guilty before God. The omission of the usual opinion is the more surprising when one sees that its implication, correctly set out, was a decisive statement on atheism. But in the description of atheism in nn. 19-21 there is so little mention of the traditional thesis that in paragraph 3 of n. 19, where the question of guilt is barely touched on in one sentence, there is only mention of the obvious fact that atheism is sinful only when man shuts out God deliberately from his heart, or, deliberately and in defiance of his conscience, evades religious questions. But nowhere does it say that a man can only be an atheist in fact by excluding God or the religious issue in such a deliberate and sinful manner.

Later on I shall speak of the possibility of an objective concept of atheism coexisting with an existentially inarticulate theism. It will then be clear that there is no contradiction between the inevitability of the religious issue and what has just been established above. The restraint of the Council with regard to the matter of guilt in atheism does not, of course, imply a minimization of atheism insofar as "the Church, as given over to the service of both God and man, cannot cease from reproving, with sorrow yet with utmost firmness, as she has done in the past, those harmful teachings and ways of acting that are in conflict with reason and with common human experience and cast man down from the noble state to which he is born" (n. 21).[6] But since the Council, Catholic pastoral theology can no longer confront the "determined" atheist with that pathetic attitude which saw in him either an ass or a criminal. It will, therefore, have to ask itself, as the Council says (n. 21), what the *real* causes are that lead to *modern* atheism, which can no longer be reduced simply to imbecility or wickedness of heart. The Council itself points to such other causes of atheism without offering a complete list nor a thoroughgoing analysis of them, and, therefore, does not dispense Catholic theology, Christian philosophy, pasto-

---

[6] For the official condemnation of atheism in earlier days, see the *Summa* referred to in the previous note, p. 20, and K. Rahner, "Atheismus (systematisch)," in *Lex f. Theol. u. Kirche*, I, p. 985 (with bibliography).

ral theology and religious pedagogics from a task that has been far from adequately tackled by these disciplines.

The Stronger Emphasis
on Potential Salvation in Atheism

The second development shown by the Council with regard to atheism, and, given the usual teaching and religious practice, liable to cause surprise, is the conviction that once we talk about an intelligible theory of atheism (to be explained later) *an atheist is not excluded from salvation on condition that his atheism has not made him act against his moral conscience.* It has already been pointed out that this condition should not be presumed and thus turn an atheist's innocence into an unrealistic hypothesis. In n. 16 of the *Constitution on the Church* we read that "those also can attain to salvation who through no fault of their own do not know the Gospel of Christ or his Church, yet sincerely seek God and moved by grace strive by their deeds to do his will as it is known to them through the dictates of conscience".[7] To this corresponds what is said in n. 22 of the *Constitution on the Church in the Modern World*: "All this sharing in Christ's resurrection holds true not only for Christians but also for all men of goodwill in whose hearts grace is active invisibly. For, since Christ died for all, and since all men are in fact called to one and the same destiny, which is divine, we must hold that the Holy Spirit offers to all the possibility of being made partners, in a way known to God, in the paschal mystery."

There is no reason why atheists should be excluded from the meaning of this statement, since this sentence refers explicitly to n. 16 of the *Constitution on the Church* where there is direct mention of those who have not reached an explicit knowledge of God. Moreover, the words, "in a way known to God", appear also in n. 7 of the *Decree on the Missionary Activity of the Church,* where a genuine possibility of supernatural faith and

[7] For this text, see the commentary by A. Grillmeier, *Das Zweite Vatikanische Konzil. Konstitutionen, Dekrete und Erklärungen. Kommentare* I (Freiburg, 1966), p. 207, with nn. 47-9 (bibl.).

salvation is recognized in the situation of the "pagan" who has not yet been touched by the Gospel. It would be arbitrary to maintain that a polytheistic pagan who, according to Paul (Eph. 2, 12),[8] is also "godless", has in principle an essentially greater chance of being saved than a modern atheist whose "personal" atheism is, after all, mainly the product of his social situation.

All these texts obviously do not assume that these atheists will still become *explicit* theists within their own understanding before they die, and that they will be saved *because* of this. If this were so, these texts would simply state the truism that an atheist can be saved when and insofar as he ceases to be an atheist. Such an interpretation would deprive the texts of any serious meaning, hardly worth a conciliar pronouncement.

Historical Significance of These Theological Differentiations

Both these points in the official teaching of the Council bring out something that is genuinely new. When we remember the explicit statements of the scriptures,[9] the traditional judgment of atheism and the cautious restraint of evangelical theology with regard to the possible salvation of the non-baptized, we cannot say that this "optimism about the salvation of non-Christians", including the atheists, was theologically obvious. The present teaching develops a line, first taken only by Pius IX (D. 5, 2865-7), which led to the declaration of August 8, 1949, of the Holy Office (DS 3866-73). But this line is here really *further* developed insofar as this "optimism about salvation" *explicitly includes atheists* in far clearer terms than was the case up till the Council.

These new explanations also go well beyond former, one might say moderately optimistic, interpretations of the situation

---

[8] For the exegesis of this text, see H. Schlier, *Der Brief an die Epheser* (Düsseldorf, 4th ed., 1963), p. 121.

[9] For a concise survey see *Lex. f. Theol. u. Kirche* I, pp. 985-6. Many scriptural statements about the fate of unbelievers should be interpreted as eschatological-prophetical "threats" with their own specific literary character much more clearly than has so far been the case in Catholic exegesis.

of non-Christians and pagans, according to which a kind of "natural" salvation was conceded for people outside the scope of Christianity (somewhat similar to the kind of salvation that Scholastic theology allowed for children that die without baptism), but which excluded them from a truly *supernatural salvation*. The *Decree on the Missionary Activity of the Church* (n. 7) states explicitly that such men can attain to a genuine saving faith through God's grace in a way we do not know more accurately, also without having accepted the explicit preaching of the Christian Gospel.[10]

Further Steps toward a Deeper Understanding

If I have stressed the two points that indicate something "new" in the pastoral constitution, I do not mean that these two points exhaust all that is new in nn. 19-21. No less important and relatively new with regard to official declarations until now are the following points that I mention without any further comments. They are: (1) the emphasis on the fact that, as the gravest phenomenon of our time, atheism requires careful examination (n. 19, par. 1; n. 21, par. 2); (2) the statement that the notion of "atheism" covers mutually very different phenomena, the causes and motives of which show an extraordinary variety among themselves (n. 19, par. 2 and 3); (3) the emphasis on the influence of sociological factors (n. 20, par. 2); (4) the reference to an existentialist atheism (n. 20, par. 1); (5) the reference to a positivist atheism which declares that the question of God is already meaningless as such (n. 19, par. 2); (6) the reference to a "postulated" atheism that sees in the absurdity of existence and the evil of the world a proof of the non-existence of God (n. 19, par. 2).

To this should be added much that has hardly been said

[10] The reference to "in a way known only to God" (n. 22 of Schema 13 gives another similar formula) about how there can be faith in such men, including atheists, does not, of course, forbid theologians to reflect on how this possibility of faith and salvation can be imagined, with the help of other theological data, without having to appeal to a miraculous divine intervention as was done in former attempts. But here we cannot further expand on this.

explicitly by the magisterium until now, such as the statement that atheism is often a denial of a God who in fact does not exist and has nothing to do with the God of the Gospel (n. 19, par. 2); the inclusion of atheists in the obligatory freedom of conscience (n. 21, par. 6); the emphasis on the possibility of a dialogue and cooperation in the world between theists and atheists; the recognition that Christians are to some extent responsible for modern atheism (n. 19, par. 3); and, lastly, all the allusions to a "mystical introduction" into the religious experience of God that go far beyond the classical proofs of God's existence in the rational manner of Scholastic philosophy and which are spread throughout these three sections of the pastoral Constitution.

III

How Can There Be a Saving Faith in an Atheist?

The two main points of the Council's teaching on atheism that I have singled out, also show up new problems and provide further insights that are important for the pastoral treatment of atheism.

The Problem

Once we have established that according to the Council's teaching an atheist is not necessarily "lost" because of his atheism, even if he dies an atheist, the theological problem arises whether "goodwill" can be a simple substitute for knowledge of God and faith in God. We have already seen that n. 7 of the *Decree on the Missionary Activity of the Church* maintains that all men can be saved, and we have included the atheist if there is no moral guilt. But the Decree says explicitly that persons, here referred to, can attain to salvation precisely because they achieve a saving *faith,* although in ways that are only known to God.[11] Therefore the question is whether and how an atheist in general can be assumed to have such a faith. One cannot answer this by simply referring to that minimum of faith[12] that traditional Scholastic theology declared to be enough under given circumstances for a supernatural, saving faith on the ground of Hebrews 11, 6.[13] This minimal faith contained already a belief in the existence of God and in God as the guarantor of the moral order. The problem can be stated in other terms: where there is faith as acceptance of divine revelation, there must be belief in *something*. Even apart from the question as to how the atheist could possibly see this "something" or content as coming through divine revelation and not merely as the fruit of a natural insight, the question remains *what* could be the object of his faith if we mean faith at all.

The conciliar texts quoted above constantly mention such an atheist as *acting according to his conscience,* as *seeking the truth,* as *fulfilling the requirements of his moral conscience.* In this way he can indeed be thought of as innocent and within reach of divine intent of salvation because, although he has not (yet) found God, he follows the demands of his conscience. But is this "content" in the awareness of an atheist enough to be the object of a *saving* faith?

With the teaching of Hebrews 11, 6 in mind one might then answer: yes, *if* this awareness contains at least implicitly a knowledge about God and if, beyond this, a free act, seized by grace, consents to this "content" in the manner of faith. Actually, this is the case. It can at least in a way be justified epistemologically. A person who sees a moral demand of his conscience as absolutely valid for him, and accepts it as such with a free act of consent, however unreflectively, affirms the absolute being

[11] For this question, see the study referred to in footnote 7.
[12] For the dogmatic aspect of this teaching, see the *Summa,* quoted in footnote 5, p. 804 (with the varying interpretations of Mitzka, Beraza and Pesch).
[13] For this, see particularly O. Michel, *Der Brief an die Hebräer* (12th ed., Göttingen, 1966), pp. 386-7; E. Grässer, *Der Glaube im Hebräerbrief* (Marburg, 1965), pp. 132ff. and elsewhere.

of God as the reason that such an *absolute moral demand* can exist *at all,* whether he knows it or not, whether he reflects upon it intelligibly or not.

Excursus on the Notion of "Knowledge of God"

We must examine this first answer somewhat more deeply. Once we assume the conscientious consent to an absolute demand, it is not very important to know how far a person reflects in this act on not only the objective but also the subjective implications of his actual knowledge and decision. It may even be that he is incapable of reflecting on such, even subjective, implications of his concrete spiritual act in intelligible objectivity. When in ordinary life a simple man acts intelligently (and this implies logically), the ultimate principles of logic are not only objectively present at the root of his intelligent insight and decision, but he has hold of them, "possesses" them spiritually, although, in his simplicity, he might be totally incapable of understanding the abstract principles of Aristotelian logic as such in their formally abstract nature, even after a certain instruction.

This simple observation taken from everyday life allows us to penetrate further into the theory and to apply it to the present question. In every act of human knowledge there are, as it were, two poles: it implies a subjective knowledge about the knower himself and the subjective aspect of his act, while at the same time this same knowledge has an object, known objectively, toward which the act is aimed and with which the act is concerned. Whenever we know something, we know something about ourselves and about our action. The objective content of such an act can also present what is unreflectively known on the subjective side of the same act, namely, when the subject, knowing himself subjectively, makes himself the object of his statement. But even in this case the dual polarity persists, the difference between the subject as subject and the subject as object of knowledge, between subjective awareness and the objectively known. Moreover, it is easily possible that such an act, which aims at a presentation of the agent himself, may still interpret this agent inadequately or falsely, although what is interpreted is present to the consciousness of the agent.

In a mental action, for example, the agent knows "subjectively" what a mental action is, since the agent-subject is present to himself with his mental action in real identity. Yet, a psychologist who holds that the senses are the ultimate source of all knowledge and in his materialistic view denies the spirituality of the subject, can, in good faith, give a wholly false theoretical interpretation of his own spiritual act. In other words, he can translate his subjective experience into an objectively false representation and formulation. Insofar as every spiritual perception and freedom constitutes a "transcendental experience" on the side of the subject and his act, i.e., an experience of the unbounded orientation of the spirit to being in general, there is, on the part of the subject, in every perception a real, though implicit, i.e., not necessarily objectively realized, perception of God—a point I cannot develop here.

What we commonly call "knowledge of God" is, therefore, not simply "the" knowledge of God but rather the objective, conceptual and articulated interpretation of what we know of God in a subjective and unreflective way. The knowledge of God is, therefore, certainly a knowledge *a posteriori* insofar as, on the one hand, the subjective act, which has always a transcendental reference to God, is an historically contingent act which, in order to exist at all, needs a real object although this is reached *a posteriori*; knowledge of God is, on the other hand, also *a posteriori* insofar as the conceptual and articulated objectivization of the transcendental experience needs to pass through the "worldly" objects of perception that are given *a posteriori*, in the sense in which the classical "proofs of God's existence" unfold this process of perception. But the knowledge of God is not *a posteriori* in the same way as happens with the perception of any outward object, such as the existence of Australia. It is true that there is no innate idea of God in the sense of an innate idea contained in the mind, but in a conceptual and articulate manner the knowledge of God is the objectification of the mind's orientation toward absolute being, implied in man's spiritual transcendental quality. This orientation is included in the experience of any spiritual act, whether of perception or of freedom, regardless of the object with which the act is concerned.

IV

The Basic Ways in Which Man Can Be Related to God

If we accept the assumptions indicated here, we can roughly draw up a list of the basic ways in which man can be related to God. We should, however, always remember that any conscious or known reality given to the spirit of man can always be freely accepted or freely rejected, since man is not merely a perceiving being, but also a free one.

First Possibility: God is given in man's transcendental character. This "givenness" is made objective in a sufficiently explicit and conceptual theism and freely accepted in the moral consent of faith (in practical life). In this case, we have that simply correct, transcendental *and* categorical theism, if I may call it thus, which is accepted by man's freedom in both dimensions and in this way affirms man's right relationship to God from every point of view. This is the kind of relationship we take for granted in a justified Christian.

Second Possibility: This transcendental and categorical theism is given and man knows and thinks correctly about God in his transcendental experience, but he rejects this perception in his moral freedom, whether he rejects God through sin or rejects him in a free act of unbelief, in the strict sense. This is the way in which we used to think, until recently, of an "atheist", when, in the religious and Christian situation, we assumed that he had somehow an objective and correct idea about God but rejected it either through sin or, beyond this, through a merely practical or both practical and theoretical "godlessness".

Third Possibility: This transcendental experience of God is given, because seen as necessary, and also freely accepted in a positive decision of the conscience, but wrongly objectified and interpreted. This inadequate, false or occasionally faulty *concept* of God can, in turn, be freely accepted or rejected, but we can leave this alone here. In any case, here we are dealing with the kind of atheism that is guiltless in the sense of Vatican Council II: an atheism at the level of categorical reflection that can coexist with a transcendental theism that is at the same time freely affirmed. Since, because of the difference between subjective transcendentality and categorical objectification in concept and formulation, transcendental theism can coexist with categorical atheism (because this difference is necessarily present in every spiritual act), there can be a guiltless atheism. This comes about, on the one hand, through the given transcendental orientation of the subject toward God, the free acceptance of this orientation, particularly in the moral act of absolute respect for the conscience and its demands, and so, through a *transcendental theism* "in the depth of the human heart", and, on the other hand, through the free rejection of the objective concept of God, i.e., a *categorical atheism* in the forefront of the reflective consciousness.

Fourth Possibility: The transcendental orientation toward God is given, but objectively wrongly or inadequately interpreted in a categorical atheism; this transcendental orientation toward God himself is freely rejected through a gravely culpable disloyalty toward one's own conscience or a culpably wrong interpretation of existence (as "totally absurd", with no absolute meaning, etc.). This free denial does not only extend to the categorical interpretation of man's transcendental being, but to being itself and so, by implication, to God. In this case we have a culpable atheism of a transcendental kind that precludes the possibility of salvation while it lasts.

These four basic types of man's relationship with God are not definitive: there are other ways of drawing up such a list, and I have myself indicated other possibilities even within this "system".

V

The Possibility of a Culpable and an Inculpable Atheism

I am mainly concerned here with showing why there can be a blameless and a guilty atheism in man; how, on the one hand, blameless atheism does not destroy every and any real basic relationship with God, which is rooted in the always present orientation of man toward God, and how, on the other hand, in spite of the possibility of a blameless atheism, the guilt of culpable atheism does not necessarily lie in the rejection of any moral imperative, but in the *ultimate* rejection of the basic orientation of man toward *God himself* and, therefore, in the free rejection of God himself.

To this must be added the categorical affirmation of God as an objective theory and decision which in no way guarantees that man takes this transcendental orientation seriously even in his free and transcendental decision. In simple words, a man, even a "Christian", can accept God objectively in his understanding and his freedom, declare that he is a "theist" and think that he observes the moral norms of God, and yet deny God in his heart either morally or as a believer. This is possible for exactly the same reason that categorical atheism can coexist with transcendental theism, equally and freely affirmed. A categorical theism can, therefore, also coexist with a transcendental theism that is freely rejected and thus be turned into a freely accepted transcendental atheism, in spite of the enduring and experienced orientation toward God.

The pastoral Constitution teaches that there is such a thing as culpable atheism, but it was not clearly explained how this is possible as really referring to God himself. It also recognized a blameless atheism without explaining clearly how this can be reconciled with faith and salvation. To understand this in theory the above-mentioned distinction between a transcendental and a categorical atheism (or theism) may be helpful. A blameless atheism will always be only a categorical atheism, an atheism on the level of conceptual and articulate objectification, where it is ultimately of no importance whether this atheistic objectification is freely accepted or rejected by man. On the other hand, a real transcendental atheism is always and necessarily culpable because God is always present in the transcendental dimension of man, and he can, therefore, not be rejected by the understanding as such but only by man's freedom. In this dimension the "object", i.e., God, is necessarily present in truth, and it is, therefore, not as if some inadequate or wrongly objectified notion of God in the dimension of categorical reflection can provide a justifiable or supposedly justifiable reason for rejection.

VI

Categorical Atheism and the Experience of God

If what has been said here, rather briefly and inadequately, has been understood, we may draw from it some pastoral indications for the right attitude of one who has to preach theism and the Gospel. This may help to explore the necessarily brief hints provided by the Council on this point. The preacher of the Gospel is never confronted by an atheist who simply has never had anything to do with God; his attitude is never that of a geography teacher who has to explain Australia to his pupil and prove that it exists. Where articulate and free human beings are concerned, the preacher of the Gospel is confronted with a man who has already a true experience of what is meant by God, but for one reason or another (blameless or culpable) is incapable of interpreting his experience of God rightly in his reflective consciousness, and so rejects the idea of God offered from "outside", either as something false or as something with which he does not know what to do. To overcome such a categorical atheism one should, therefore, never stay on this level, nor bring up proofs of God's existence as if these could be treated with the same procedure and method as the proof for the existence of an object that can only be approached through a purely *a posteriori* experience and is therefore rightly rejected by such a person at the outset as of no interest to him and unworthy of his personal and spiritual exertions.

Even when one has to talk to an atheist on the level of the familiar "proofs of God's existence", the success of such a conversation will today inevitably depend on whether the atheist has been made aware of his own experience of God in a kind of "mystical instruction". When he really knows about unconditional loyalty, absolute truthfulness, unselfish commitment to the good of others and similar basic human attitudes, then he knows something about God, even if not reflectively. In concrete individual cases it may, of course, be very difficult to make the theological implications of such attitudes clear in a reflective and objective way. The attempt may even fail in such a concrete case, but this is no more astonishing than when one fails to explain the formal logic in theoretical reflection to someone who nevertheless uses it in his daily life and understands things *in* this everyday logic. In any case, the usual proofs of God's existence can only be used fruitfully with someone who is not already a "theist", if the rational argument is linked with such a "mystical instruction". Accordingly, one should also examine the difficulties which, according to the Constitution, give rise to the various forms of contemporary atheism: the resentment of evil in the world, the supposed failure of every religious experience, the supposed threat to man by the idea of God, peculiar presentations that someone may link with the idea of God, etc.

When we understand what is meant by that transcendental theism mentioned above, it is also clear that for a genuine theist God himself is not given in the framework of our everyday experience in the same way as other objects of our *a posteriori* experiences. He is not some being within the framework of our experience, but always the prior condition to our transcendental dimension. A theist or an apologist of theism should, therefore, never pretend that, although God cannot be directly seized by

the experience of our senses, he can nevertheless be recognized in the way one can conclude to the existence of an electric current, invisible in itself from its effects. This is the point where we can understand that phenomenon of atheism to which the Council refers when it says that some atheists remain fixed in a "phenomenalism of science" and think that they can in no way understand what is meant by the word "God".

The right understanding of the nature of the knowledge of God cannot be concerned with an attempt to broaden and deepen the scope of empirical experience by the use of its own methods. It is rather a matter of bringing man to the understanding of the fact that there is a wholly different, even a transcendental experience in spiritual knowledge and in freedom where what we mean by "God" can be understood and perceived as real; and also the fact that what we mean by this transcendental, God-oriented experience is the very condition that makes every *a posteriori* experience of everyday life and of science possible, even though it is not, and cannot be, the task of these sciences, based on *a posteriori* experiences, to reflect upon this prior condition.

Vatican Council I declared explicitly (cf. DS 3001) that God is incomprehensible. No Christian teaching about God and his knowability has ever denied this. But in practice our explanation of theism has often forgotten this dogma. One can really not say that we know God just as we know something in the fact and manner of its existence, and then attribute to this known God the quality of being incomprehensible. The proof of God and, therefore, the necessary "mystical instruction" must from the start point to the absolute mystery[14] that governs our whole existence; we must then bring it closer to theoretical knowledge and the existential fulfillment of life, and then say: "This is really what we mean by 'God'."

[14] Cf. K. Rahner, "Uber den Begriff des Geheimnisses in der katholischen Theologie," in *Schriften zur Theologie* IV (4th ed., Einsiedeln, 1964), pp. 51-99.

VII

The Seriousness of the Atheistic Question
for Pastoral Work

In the *Pastoral Constitution on the Church in the Modern World*, Vatican Council II has pointed out in the most emphatic way that contemporary atheism requires new and most serious thought of the Church and those who preach the Gospel. Such a declaration should not remain a pious formula, part of that store of courtesies one reserves for an opponent. There are really questions that demand a new formulation and a new reply, if we really want to engage in a genuine dialogue with contemporary atheism. These questions are not merely concerned with the way in which we can best approach the modern atheist "didactically" or "pedagogically". These questions touch the essence of the matter. Therefore, the pastoral-theological question of how to approach modern atheism[15] becomes very soon the question of what is really meant by "God" himself and of how we, as theists and Christians, have acquired access originally to this incomprehensible mystery of our existence. This mystery sustains us and at the same time makes us question ourselves. This access[16] can no longer be taken for granted through sociological circumstances. Through it we can speak among Christians of God, and think we know *who* we are and *why* our own life would be meaningless *without God*. When we affirm this, we announce an ultimate truth of our life, but we have understood it ourselves only when at the same time we *experience* this life as meaningful. And so we face the question whether we accept or reject this experienced meaning. In this experience and its acceptance, we know what is really meant by "God".

[15] Cf. the article by K. Lehmann, "Some Ideas from Pastoral Theology on the Proclamation of the Christian Message to Present-Day Unbelievers," in this volume of *Concilium*.

[16] For this question, see K. Rahner, "Frömmigkeit—früher und heute," in *Schriften zur Theologie* VII (Einsiedeln, 1966).

Charles Moeller/*Rome, Italy*

The Theology of Unbelief

An Hypothesis for the Principles Underlying the Salvific Action of the Church

I

THE "HIDDEN GOD"

The "theology" of unbelief: the terms, as such, are themselves contradictory. To speak even of a "theology" of schism is already a paradox. How much more so when it is a question of unbelief, which stands in direct contradiction to theology or the teaching about God.

In reality, it is better to speak of the sense, or the meaning, that the fact of unbelief can have for a believer, and especially for a Christian living in the Church. Paul VI has said that atheism is one of most serious realities of our day. It is fitting, therefore, for us to inquire into its inner meaning, and attempt for pastoral theology what Jean Lacroix has already done from the philosophical point of view when he spoke of the "meaning of modern atheism".[1]

In the words of Julian Green, the faith in the Middle Ages seemed "to move forward under its own momentum": "but now", he adds, "we live in a world where doubt has become the normally accepted attitude". Pastoral theology cannot just dismiss unbelief as an unfortunate "accident". It is only too real a fact which must be taken into consideration in any approach to

[1] J. Lacroix, *Le sens de l'athéisme moderne* (Tournai: Casterman, 1958).

25

the apostolate. All are agreed about this, but often the problem is treated on merely a superficial level.

Although it may disturb some people, I will say at the very beginning that what is new is not unbelief as such, but rather the fact that it is now treated as a problem or a new dimension, as a sociological condition to be studied in itself. The fact of unbelief is not something new. There have always been men who did not believe. Looking deeper into the problem, a permanent temptation to unbelief gnaws at the heart of the unbeliever himself. In the bible there is a never ending struggle against every form of idolatry. All too often we forget this constant preaching and reiterated proclamation of the prophets about the one *true* God, whom we continually degrade into idols fashioned by our own hands.

Today it is often said that "God cannot be understood of himself". In this connection there is no longer any "Selbstverständlichkeit". This can mean two things: that we live in a *society* that is no longer "sacral", that does not "lead" us to God; a society where the normal thing would be to believe. We have already spoken of this above, and it is only too true. But it can also mean that God is not *evident,* that he cannot be "comprehended", that he is to be found only at the end of an exhaustive inquiry into the whole of being. Here, unconsciously, we are touching on the biblical and conciliar themes about the God "who dwells in light inaccessible", the *Deus incomprehensibilis,* the Greek *aperileptos,* mentioned by St. John Chrysostom and Vatican Council I.

It is important not to confuse the principles of sociology with the approaches adopted by metaphysics and theology. The "negative" theology of Pseudo-Dionysius or Gregory of Nyssa, all that St. Thomas said about the God of whom we know far more about what he is not than what he "is", what John of the Cross wrote about the "night of the senses and the spirit" are all instances of this search for the "hidden God" spoken of so magnificently by Isaiah. At the very heart of his revelation God lies hidden. "One cannot see God without death", says

the Pentateuch. "God, no man has ever seen him", is the message of St. John. And yet, Deuteronomy can say that "God spoke to Moses like a friend speaks to his friend"; and St. John goes on to say: "The only Son, who is in the bosom of the Father, he has made him known".

So it is in the paradox of the "cloud" which during the day is darkened, but shines brilliantly at night, that God both reveals himself and lies hidden. He remains hidden and inaccessible— "superessential" in the words of Gregory of Nyssa—in the depths of his revelation. That is why the same Gregory of Nyssa could take the life of Abraham with its central *leitmotif*: "Leave thy country behind thee and come away into the land I will show to thee" as the image and the type of that exodus through which man must journey ceaselessly into the depths of the God-head.

Perhaps the first lesson of unbelief is to remind us of the "inaccessibility" of God.[2]

II

THE PHENOMENOLOGY OF CONTEMPORARY UNBELIEF

It will be useful to point out the difference of meaning between unbelief and atheism. The expression "atheism" of itself implies a kind of systematization; it has an abstract quality about it. No doubt the word "unbelief" indicates the same central attitude —that of denying God—but here the approach is more concrete, envisaging the person much more than the system. Thus, on the one hand, the study is more systematic, on the other, more phenomenological.

It is, however, important not to lose sight of the different possible kinds of atheism, for it is helpful to classify the attitudes that people assume in practice into definite patterns of thought.

[2] J. Daniélou, *Platonisme et théologie mystique. Grégoire de Nysse* (Coll. Théologie 3, Paris, 1949).

Otherwise they would be lost in an infinity of possible shadings of emphasis without our ever being able to appreciate their basic underlying tendencies.

1. *The Theoretical Approach*

There is *negative* and *positive* atheism. The first is the atheism of those who do not accept that the existence of God can be stated as a definite fact. Very often we find this associated with *agnosticism,* which in a writer like Duhamel is tinged with "nostalgia", with despair in Roger Martin du Gard, and a mixture of distrust and resentment in Albert Camus.

Positive atheism is that which denies God so as to be able to affirm man. "God is dead, *and so* man is born", said Malraux, paraphrasing Nietzsche. In the words of Sartre: "Atheism is a humanism." "The moral conscience dies on contact with the absolute", according to Merleau-Ponty.[3]

The expression "antitheism" is also sometimes used. But in our opinion this notion is of only a marginal value for the understanding of the problem of unbelief. Either it means a rejection of a God *who is known,* and, unfortunately, such rejection is an only too real tragedy, one of those dramas where a man chooses nothingness, as we have been made so aware of in some of the characters that Dostoievski and Bernanos have portrayed for us;[4] or else it means the rejection of an idol, some mere caricature of God. This kind of rejection can be colored by a variety of human reactions and feelings where pride plays its part; but then in that case we are no longer dealing with unbelief as such.

Following on a suggestion made by Jean Lacroix, we can say that atheism can be "scientific" when it is bound up with a certain interpretation of the exact sciences; it is "political", for example, in its Marxist form; and can be described as "moral" when it

[3] A. Dondeyne, *La foi écoute le monde* (Louvain, 1964) goes into greater detail.
[4] C. Moeller, "Aspects de l'athéisme dans la littérature moderne," in *L'ateismo contemporaneo,* to appear under the editorship of P. J. Girardi.

is the basis of humanism or the assertion of man.[5] Thus, we see in the pages of Jules Romains examples of scientific atheism, in the work of Bertolt Brecht examples of political atheism, and examples of moral atheism in Simone de Beauvoir.[6]

When Simone de Beauvoir lost her childhood faith, she said that she felt as if she had "passed from the heaven of ideas to the earth of men"; and we can take this as a particularly apposite summary of the central principle of contemporary atheism. In other words, atheism today is just as much characterized by an affirmation of man himself as by the denial of God, and can thus be described as "anthropological" atheism.[7]

2. The Practical Approach

Only rarely is one of these forms of atheism found in its "pure" state; on the other hand, there are innumerable "mixed varieties". The sociological, psychological and cultural study of the different forms of unbelief has hardly begun. Thus, in the unbelief of Camus there is a very complex core of agnosticism and resentment; in other words, there is evidence as much of the influence of Taine as that of Nietzsche.[8]

In this connection we must speak of *"practical atheism"*, which means the denial of God implied in the actual life of those who profess to believe in him. There is also unbelief through *indifference*: "God? Why I never give him a thought," was how Françoise Sagan summed this up in an interview. We can also speak of *sociological* unbelief induced by the particular cultural background: very often here the attitude is not so much the result of reflection, but merely the consequence of social pressures.

[5] This threefold division is taken from Jean Lacroix; cf. *supra,* footnote 1.

[6] C. Moeller, *Littérature du XXe siècle et christianisme, Amour humain,* will include a study on Brecht and another on Simone de Beauvoir.

[7] A. Vergote, *Psychologie religieuse* (Coll. Psychologie et sciences humaines, Brussels, 1966), pp. 277-84.

[8] The influence of Nietzsche even today in the matter of unbelief cannot be exaggerated.

III

THE HERMENEUTIC OF UNBELIEF

We use the expression here in the sense of a "reading in depth", prescinding entirely from its exegetical connotation.[9] It seems that from this point of view there are *three possible and complementary approaches*. Each envisages the entirety of the phenomenon of present unbelief, but each does so according to a different criterion. In other words, we are not talking about approaches at progressively different levels, but of alternative and mutually complementary insights.

1. *Explicit Unbelief*

This means the absence of any clearly expressed faith. The writing of Sartre is "explicitly" atheistic: in it the idea of God is presented as contradictory. We have already mentioned that for the author of *Being and Nothingness* atheism is in fact a humanism. Furthermore one has only to read *The Devil and the Good Lord*—where at the end Goetz says: "Joy, tears of joy. There is no God. The sky is empty,"—to feel oneself in the presence of an utterly explicit unbelief, at least in the chief character of the work. The world of Ingmar Bergmann is another example of explicit unbelief. When, at the end of *Smiles of a Summer Night* Maria, the young girl who has just lost her student lover in a senseless accident, asks her uncle "whether God is interested in her love story", he replies that "God has other things to do than concern himself with the love stories of young people"; thereupon she says: "If God is not concerned about me, I have no longer any interest in him; I spit in his face".

2. *Underlying Motivations*

The most emphatic and explicit statements are not always the most genuine. We must also discover the underlying motivation, or, better still, the "basic feeling about life" (*Grundgefühl*). It would appear, for instance, that in Marcel this is a feeling of

[9] P. Ricoeur, *De l'interprétation? Essai sur Freud* (Paris, 1965), pp. 521ff.

exile: the man who experiences life as an exile—for example he who asks himself "what has become of once loved persons"— bears witness to some native land, no doubt now lost, but whose presence haunts him, "like some buried Atlantis". On the other hand, Sartre's characters see life as a *threat,* or trap, and this even deep down at the very heart of those things that at first sight seem to invite our trust and confidence, like the affection of a grandfather for his grandchild. J. Rivière experiences life under the symbol of a void, of nothingness, just like Unamuno, Pascal and Pirandello. And on the other hand, Du Bos and Henry Alain-Fournier interpret life under the symbol of *plenitude.*

Very often, no doubt, some particular *event* or incident lies at the root of an expressedly avowed unbelief. Camus, as he stands before the body of the little Arab boy crushed by a motor bus, points to the blue sky and says to his friend: "You see, the sky is dumb": here we see an example of a profound traumatic experience, all the more so that it took place when he was only fifteen. The frightening blasphemy of Maria in *Smiles of a Summer Night* is repetition or re-enactment of an experience that Bergmann lived through when he was sixteen.

As has often been said, incidents like these reveal the deepest levels of a person's emotional life; as they strike to the very depths of the personality, they betray that person's basic feeling about life.

Here it has been necessary, in order to throw light on the pastoral problem, to indicate the main groups of mental attitudes in this matter of unbelief. In fact, since it is a question of the Church's approach in its proclamation of salvation, it is vital always to take into account these deep underlying structures of man's affective nature.[10]

3. *The Hermeneutic of Symbols*

Another approach is possible which we derive from literature, among other sources, but which contributes greatly to an under-

---

[10] This basic motivation, itself rooted in the fundamental understanding of life, is all the time being more appreciated as vital to the whole problem.

standing of real life. We refer to the great *symbols* whose presence
(or absence) in a work confer upon it either a religious or a-
religious meaning. In fatherhood—as law, model and promise[11]
—culpability and consolation we have three themes which together are either witnesses to some archaic and vestigial memory
of childhood that still casts its paralyzing spell upon us, or a
symbol pointing a way to some message of universal validity
embodying certain essential characteristics of the religious problem.[12]

In this sense, the meaning of James Joyce's writing is quite
clear and explicit. But if an approach is made to it from a
different point of view—a reading with insight, as Marcel would
say—we can detect in it an underlying symbolic meaning.
Ulysses, for example, is the story of the father's search. In the
microcosm which is Dublin and (which is) also the little Jewish
clerk, Leopold Bloom, it presents the whole history of the
world, all the "once upon a times" of all the stories. But
throughout the whole work runs a hidden thread of meaning,
namely, that it is the severing of the bond of paternal generation
which is at the root of the kind of chaos, the essential "non-sense"
in which all the characters live.

We find the same in T. S. Eliot's *Elder Statesman.* Behind the
description of a slightly crazy English guest house and the sort
of confession made by a father to his daughter, we can detect
the Greek myth of Oedipus. The peace which glows through the
old man at the gates of Athens is reflected in the peace that
shines through Lord Claverton after he has confessed the sins
of his youth to his daughter, Monica, the new Antigone. But
that is not all; there is also a Christian meaning there, which
can be described as that of fatherhood, rediscovered in the confession of his human failings and which enables us to catch a
glimpse of peace that surpasses understanding.

[11] Cf. A. Vergote, *op. cit. supra* footnote 7, pp. 199ff.
[12] This is well brought out in Resnais—Duras's film (and text) *Hiro-
shima mon amour.* It shows the frustration of a search intended to explore
the future, but which turns aside into forgetfulness.

Finally, as a third example, in certain passages of Sartre's *Condemned of Altona,* behind the obsessive domination of a dictatorial and arbitrary father, we can sense the true image of a father who judges and restores life.[13]

You may perhaps ask what value these literary approaches have. For our part, we consider them to be most illuminating, because they show that *atheists are perhaps not always those whom we think.* If Sartre's work is deeply and explicitly anti-religious—and we must never lose sight of this more obvious aspect—it perhaps also reveals other aspects where an openness to a religious viewpoint is at least possible. In *Words,* for example, all can see that we have, by contrast, a description of the Word of God. Through the caricature Sartre draws of "the words" in which the family lives, we catch a glimpse of what the true Word which creates, re-creates, saves and judges would be.[14]

Therefore, our "hermeneutic" or reading in depth is important. Here we are not talking about giving transcendental value judgments, but rather seeking for a new *pastoral* approach. Becoming aware of this threefold, complementary approach in a work of literature, helps us to realize that the same approach can be used when dealing with souls which are apparently shut tight in unbelief.

And more especially, the searching out of the original experience, which so often lies at the root of a loss of faith, and, above all, the detection of a person's basic feeling about life can be of considerable help in our preaching the Good News of salvation. Those whose religious avowals are the most definite and explicit are not always the most religious. In this respect, Claudel's writing presents some curious anomalies. On the

[13] We refer to the last scene in Act V when Franz throws himself into the arms of his father, who presses him to himself, saying: "My poor, little child." There are not many scenes of this kind in Sartre's work, and so this short episode seems to have a deeper significance.

[14] Sartre's work *Words* is, without doubt, the most revealing he has published up to the present. We have published a study of this work in the ninth edition of *La Foi en Jesus Christ* (Casterman, 1965).

other hand, some who are far removed from us are, in fact, much closer than we think. To see this, we need only consider the writing of Proust, where we see a gradual discovery of the meaning of duration under the symbol of memory, and then very soon, of time as something to be redeemed, through the sense of moral responsibility binding us to those who have loved us.[15]

In other words, some human "worlds" might appear to be open, and yet are actually shut tight; whereas others in some mysterious way are open, even when we have the evidence of explicit statements that indicate the contrary. The world of Antonioni appears indifferent to the problem of God: no one ever speaks of it. And, in fact, this is a closed world. In it men are held captive by the elements of this world: they are a prey to the slightest movements of their "animal spirits", which, at the end of the "venture", force them to do the direct opposite of what they wanted to do at the outset (cf. *L'avventura*). By contrast, the world of Bergmann remains "open", for, at least, it is a world of enigma and doubt. But all the time, beneath the surface, we sense a preoccupation with the religious question, which helps us to a better understanding of works like *Through a Glass Darkly*.

IV

THE UNDERLYING MOTIVATIONS OF PRESENT UNBELIEF

We shall now attempt to map out the *underlying* motives of unbelief. Indeed we are of the opinion that what lies below the surface is often more enlightening than what is explicit. We trust that what we have said so far has shown this.

[15] A study on Proust from this point of view will be included in the seventh tome of our *Littérature du XXe siècle et christianisme*. In the meantime, our brief sketch in *Religion et littérature: esquisse d'une méthode de lecteur* (Comparative Literature Studies, 2, 4, 1965, University of Maryland), pp. 330-2, may be consulted.

1. *The Rejection of Dualism*

Nietzsche said that Christianity is "a Platonism for the people". This maxim should always be born in mind, like the equally famous one of Marx about the opium of the people. "It is clear", writes G. Morel, "that a whole pessimistic, withdrawn and puritanical tradition has penetrated to the depths of Western man's consciousness". And he quotes these lines from Sean O'Casey: "How much time has been lost since the origin of man in striving to know what the other world will be like! The more earnest the effort expended in this direction, the less man knew about the present world in which he lived . . . But when we say that this must be our home, there is nothing sad about this. Even if it could only afford us a simple shelter and our barest needs in clothing and food, but adding to this the lily and the rose, the apple and the pear, it would still be a home for man, whether he is mortal or immortal." [16]

No need to mention Freud's argument in *Future of an Illusion*. It is only a variant of the main objection, namely, that religion robs man of his dignity and integrity, forcing him to transfer the energies and responsibilities, for which he is entirely accountable, to another world projected by his own misguided and deceived conscience.

2. *The Denial of the "God of Nature"*

A long time ago, Father Sertillanges said that the "God who is dead" is not the true living God, but the God of nature. At present a whole "divine cosmology", a whole approach to the divinity through the "signs of nature", in itself quite admirable, is going through a phase of critical reappraisal. Urs von Balthasar has shown how the centuries of "Christian stoicism" are now giving way before the discovery of man's solitude and responsibility in face of the world. No longer can man feel himself "wrapped around" by his mother Nature, where some sort of

[16] Quoted by G. Morel, "Les images de Dieu," in *Dieu d'aujourd'hui* (Paris, 1965), p. 188.

benign and gracious divinity is present and visible for all to see.[17]

But it is not only the cosmos that has been "desacralized" in this way: this is also true of the world of men. During the past ten years everything has been said about *"secularization"*, the process by which the society once sacralized through the Christian establishment is now once more being placed back into the hands of men.[18] Proudhon wanted to be "antitheistic" through theism; he wanted, in fact, to "defatalize" man's destiny and to restore to him the consciousness of his own responsibility.[19]

3. *Distrust of Religious and Mystical Experience*

Malègue had seen that modern man believes only in experience. His conclusion was that in some sort of way the Absolute must become visible in what we experience. So an essential aspect of his writing, especially in *Terres noires, Les classes moyennes du salut,*[20] was designed to show the flowering of the godlike quality of the Christian faith in the lives of simple people, whom he describes as "the middle classes of sanctity".

Modern man distrusts religious experience. He sees in it a kind of emotional reverie, consisting of a nostalgia and a fear in face of reality which is construction and destruction. He sees in it the continuance of the infantile memory of plenitude in the mother's womb: the "sentiment océanique", which Romain Rolland speaks of in his celebrated letter to Freud, is really nothing more than a regression toward the archaic and prelogical.

More generally, from this point of view, God appears as the projection of the father who protects—a protecting father figure. He is seen as the one dispensing man from responsibility of free choice in time of difficulty and danger.[21]

[17] H. Urs von Balthasar, *Dieu et l'homme d'aujourd'hui* (Paris: Desclée, 1959).

[18] The most recent book is H. Cox, *The Secular City* (New York, 1965).

[19] H. de Lubac, *Proudhon et le catholicisme* (Paris, 1943).

[20] In the second tome, 9th edition, of our *Littérature du XXe siècle et christianisme: La foi en Jesus Christ,* we have added a long study on this book.

[21] Cf. A. Vergote, *op. cit.* p. 155.

4. Ineffectiveness and Uselessness of God

Dieu, pourquoi faire?, you may remember, was the title of a book which aroused considerable attention in its day. The uselessness of the God "of explanation", brought in to explain the phenomena of the world, is one of the basic assumptions of science as it grows in awareness of its own power and potential.[22]

Also the apparent failure of God to change the world, to ward off worldwide disaster, and then "the silence of God" convince many people of his uselessness and ineffectiveness. There is no doubt a marked tendency to judge God on the sole level of his effectiveness. Cardinal Suhard said: "Man must be grafted upon God, and not God upon man"; and yet, at the same time, does it not seem that sometimes God has been cut down to the level of secondary causes? a sort of children's nurse whose sole reason for existence is to ward off catastrophe?

V

ELEMENTS FOR THE CHURCH'S PREACHING
OF THE GOSPEL OF SALVATION

Now that we have examined the basic motivations underlying present unbelief—humanism, secularization, realism and responsibility—we can sketch out the broad outline of a proclamation of salvation by the Church.

1. The Hidden God

The theme with which we began this essay now reappears, but in a different perspective. There is no doubt that among all God's attributes special emphasis must be placed today on his transcendence. The experience of the desert is basic to the revelation of the Old Law, and still remains essential in the New. Modern man often ridicules believers because of the indescribably narrow conception they have of God: they would prefer a "much greater"

[22] Cf. J. Lacroix, *op. cit.* the section on scientific atheism.

God. God's silence, far from being the sign of his non-existence, is rather one of the paradoxical signs of his reality: "In a de-sacralized world, but one which still bears the marks of the Other, God remains silent. But silence," as Bernanos remarked, "is a characteristic quality of God. Indeed, the estrangement between man, the sacred and God leaves room for another presence: that of the Word of the Wholly Other." [23] This expresses in modern language the teaching of biblical revelation about the "hidden God".

2. *The God of Hope*

In view of the distrust of "religious" experience, and especially because of the type of criticism that sees in the religious approach —what tradition calls the "desire for God"—a regressive nostalgia for the plenitude of infancy, it is important to be most definite about the fact that faith is not a regression or a return to some lost paradise; instead, it is a looking to the future, a projection forward of one's whole being. Faith is the foundation of hope. Christian hope is not a survival of primitive feelings of delight and pleasure from which we are unable to break ourselves away.

But it must be said, at the same time, that this experience of plenitude is something absolutely fundamental. As such, it is "pre-religious": we must move beyond it, but in such a way that the content of initial experience is perfectly integrated into our personalities. The truth of this can be seen from the fact that when this has not taken place there is always a most serious and permanent psychological deficiency.

When we assume the "pre-religious" past in this way, it means that the past is present within us at this moment, and, once it is integrated by it, is projected toward the future. Hence, the profundity of Paul Ricoeur's remark: *"Hope is the same thing as remembering"*. Indeed, it shows that if there is one way of remembering, which is a drawing in of the person within himself, a life spent looking backward—as we find, for example, in a series of episodes in Proust's writings—there is another way, inspired

[23] A. Vergote, *op. cit.*, p. 94.

by the Platonic recollection, which far from being closed in upon itself is, in fact, open to the future. Thus, once it has been rediscovered, accepted and, when it is a question of moral experience, also *judged,* the past no longer weighs upon us as an obsession with past pleasures and moral culpability, but once disentangled, brought out into the open and transformed as a result of this judgment, now shares in our hope.[24] Then we can turn Paul Ricoeur's aphorism around and say that *"remembering is the same thing as hope":* and it thus becomes clear that Christian hope in no respect is a seeking for some "belle au bois dormant". Can we not see here the same line of thought as that pursued by St. Paul who, when treating of original sin, goes back from the second Adam to the first, and also the way that the Council of Trent speaks of original sin—the "past" of the human race—directly in a redemptive context.[25]

We are here in line with the promise, expectation and hope. We assume what the psychologists call "the principle of reality"; we discover faith and the hope of salvation in the context of a confrontation with reality in seeking and searching. Using the vocabulary of religious psychology, we could say that we are assuming at the same time the principle of totality and the principle of reality.

3. *God Who Creates Man in His Own Image*

This aspect corresponds to the first two underlying motivations of unbelief that we called "humanism" and "secularization".

Here the teaching of the bible on God as the Father and creator is central. Creation is also a communication, because God created man in his own image. The text from Genesis, of vital importance in the *Pastoral Constitution on the Church in the Modern World,* means, among other things, that God has made man a creature who must have dominion over the world. The words: "let us make man in our own image" *and* that "he

[24] P. Ricoeur, *Finitude et culpabilité* (Paris, 1960), pp. 218-43.
[25] M. Labourdette. *Le péché originel et les origines de l'homme* (Paris, 1953).

has dominion over the birds of the air", etc., really mean, *"that is to say,* that he might have dominion . . ." In other words, at the heart of biblical anthropology, we discover man being summoned and called by God to submit the world to his control. So the responsibility and the autonomy of man before the universe that he must transform are engraven deeply into the pattern of revelation itself.

No doubt man must also be the "servant of God"; he must be at the service of his brethren. Even more, he must suffer, accepting death and suffering, all the labors of life that are just as clearly written into his destiny as his summons to dominate the world.

But here, precisely, Jesus Christ, the Messiah, has been the model and example: the *New Adam* became the *Servant of Yahweh;* he was "obedient unto death, even the death of the cross". And that is why "he was exalted above every other name". In other words, the exemplary image of man is the risen Jesus, the glorified humanity of the incarnate Word. The stigmata borne by the human body of Jesus show that the image of the Servant of God is an essential part of the picture of the exaltation of Christ in glory.

Is there any need to remind ourselves that here we have a quite evident and absolutely central principle? The Servant of God was raised in glory, not in spite of his obedience, but through it and because of it.

At the same time, the theme of "secularization" is seen in its true perspective. Man confronted with the world is commanded by God to harness it into the service of man, with the intention of bringing it within the human orbit. The contradiction between "secularization" and "sacralization" is thus transcended. To enliven the world with the spirit of Christ does not necessarily mean introducing it in that particular form of Christian civilization that was embodied in the society of the Middle Ages, although, at the same time, there were in this civilization certain stable and permanent elements that transcended the particular shape it took at that period in history. The fact of being created by God is the foundation of man's freedom and even of his responsibility. If, then, in the autonomy essential to the self-awareness of modern man, there is a continual danger of Promethean revolt, there is also a way which, in the light of the creation in the image of God, opens up toward a harmony of the human and the divine. Here again it is Christ who is the model.[26]

4. *The Word of God*

Paul Ricoeur has shown how the great religious penitential texts in the Old Testament are a "Word" incarnating the law, the model to follow and also the promise of life. In them a peremptory question is put to man. More especially, the Word of God appears as that which causes a complete break with the nostalgic memories of childhood; it judges, proclaiming the law, saying what is good and bad, and at the same time restoring life to us. Freud was not able to grasp this dimension of the biblical texts which, otherwise, he had studied so intently. Finally, the Word brings about a face-to-face confrontation between man and God, thus showing the personal character of the divinity.[27]

VI

Prophetic and Eschatological Affirmation

All that has been said so far was designed as an outline for a preparation for the preaching of the Gospel, based on the sociological and psychological facts relating to contemporary unbelief. There we saw the assertion of God's existence as a response and answer. But it is also a moving beyond, for in the unforeseen, indeed, in the transcendent nature of this affirmation, its truth takes on a new dimension.

We should like to conclude this article by considering this latter aspect in greater detail, for we consider it as being perhaps the most important.

[26] H. Urs von Balthasar, *op. cit.* develops this theme *passim;* cf. A. Vergote, *op. cit.,* pp. 244-62.
[27] A. Vergote, *op. cit.,* pp. 262ff.

1. *God's Summons and Human Choice*

We must never forget that God is not a problem, but a "mystery", to use Gabriel Marcel's expression. In other words, God is not an object, a possession, something standing before me, that I can seize hold of or not, or whose presence I can verify. He is the mystery that cannot be defined, in whom I, in some sort of way, "am", and who entirely changes my life according to whether he is or is not.[28]

In other words, we must always remember that to believe or not to believe in God implies a choice, a complete "conversion". We must never lose sight of this fact, although today there is a growing tendency to do just that. Blondel has shown how the apparent "determinism" of the dialectic of action was completely dependent—as it were, suspended from above—on the choice made before the one necessary thing: to be gods along with God, or to be gods without God.[29]

The Church must never lose sight of this approach to unbelief. Here the Word of God rediscovers its full prophetic significance. It must always produce a kind of dissolution, an uprooting, an entry into a completely new world that "the ear has not heard, that the eye has never seen, nor that has ever entered into the heart of man". But we must not be deceived: the very newness of the Word, what we might call its existential impact, along with the attraction of a summons and a new freedom, also stimulates a kind of mobilization of the forces within a man whose influence is exerted in persuading him not "to leave his country, his parents and his whole substance".

2. *"A Confessing Community"*

In the same line of thought, we must never forget that the present-day world experiences the reality of progress and power

---

[28] We have studied this aspect of Marcel's work in *Littérature du XXe siècle et christianisme IV: L'esperance en Dieu Notre Père* (Tournai, 1965).

[29] This is the central point in Blondel's first work. Cf. our study on Blondel in *Au seuil du christianisme* (Coll. Cahiers de Lumen Vitae, no. I, Brussels, 1948).

just as much as that of non-sense and the absurd. In the face of this situation, Christianity appears as a proclamation of the *ultimate meaning of things*. "The modern world," writes Paul Ricoeur, "can be viewed under the twofold sign of a growing rationality along with a growing absurdity. We discover that men certainly lack justice and, most assuredly, love, but even more they lack meaning: the meaninglessness of work, leisure and sexuality—these are the problems that we encounter today. Faced with these problems, our task is not one of recrimination or regret: the function of the believing community is to be a witness and representative of some fundamental meaning. . . . You might ask: why are Christians needed for this responsibility? I do not say that others could not bear this burden; but I do say that the Christian has his own reasons for doing so; the proclamation of the death and resurrection of Christ helps him to see the surplus of sense over non-sense in history. In the words of St. Paul: 'Where sin abounds, there grace superabounds.' Being a Christian means detecting the signs of this superabundance in the very order that the human race expresses its own designs. The Christian stands as the adversary of the absurd and the prophet of the meaning of things. Not through some despairing act of the will, but through a recognition of the fact that this meaning has been made clear in the events proclaimed by scripture. He will never finish the task of spelling out and forming a complete picture of this inner meaning." [30]

But this proclamation must take place in a *liturgical, ecclesial community*. "The subject of faith is 'we' not 'I'. It is through the 'we' that the transmission or the tradition, in the literal sense of the word, is carried on. The Word arouses and stimulates men only when it continues to be transmitted, and the purpose of preaching is to be heard by many. . . . The dialectic of conviction and responsibility must be supported by the more profound dialectic of the ecclesial and the social." [31]

[30] P. Ricoeur, "Science humaine et conditionnement de la foi," in *Dieu aujourd'hui* (Paris, 1965), pp. 140-1.
[31] *Ibid*. p. 142.

Consequently, we must dissociate ourselves entirely from the kind of identification of the Church and the world sought today by many in the movement for the secularization of Christianity.[32] The Church must always remain a liturgical and cultic community, so that, among its other means of showing itself to the world, it might appear as the messenger of hope, *issued from God,* in Jesus Christ, saving the world, but also transcending it, transfiguring it and purifying it. "The idea that the Church loses itself in the world," continues Paul Ricoeur, "makes no sense to me; for if it is lost without trace, there is nothing more that can be lost. The function, not only of preaching, but of worship also, is to maintain an inner sanctum where a grip on the true meaning and 'sense' of reality can be preserved, so that the outward dialectic between the Church and the world can be fostered. Worship, here, is a specific action, a *praxis* enveloping the Word, an action which is 'useless', neither social, economic nor technological, but where the symbolism of the Word is seen through the symbolism of gesture and action. It is in worship that a community, a 'we', is born and continues to reproduce itself." [33]

Worship is, of course, much more than a witness of faith; but it is also that as well. The "apostolic" mission of the Church in proclaiming God in its *worship* always remains at the center of its message.

VII

CONCLUSION: MYSTERY OF SALVATION

Both of these approaches, preparation for the Gospel and prophetic proclamation, are equally important. Each adds something to and complements the other. Here again we must speak of a *convergence* at the very heart of the mystery of salvation.

The *mystery of salvation:* here we probably come to the central reality. Modern man asserts that he has no need for salvation;

[32] E. Mascall, *The Secularization of Christianity* (London, 1963) is one of the first critical studies—perhaps a little one-sided—on certain aspects of this movement.

[33] P. Ricoeur, *art. cit.* p. 142.

he sees in this "non-necessity" the very foundation of his own dignity and responsibility as man. And yet, at the same time, he is the one whose whole history shouts out the need for some salvation, some meaning and some underlying sense to his life.

In this rejection of salvation, there are many false presuppositions. Too often salvation is seen by those who reject it as an unwelcome gift that implies the slavery and subjection of the one who receives it. And very often those who believe in salvation, without always being conscious of the fact, project an idea of it as being nothing more than a superficial addition to our lives shielding us from the abyss of death and suffering, as Bergson has so well shown in *Two Sources of Morality and Religion,* in connection with introverted morality and static religion.[34]

Perhaps, today there is no other subject whose study and detailed examination is more important than that of the mystery of salvation. It must be approached from every angle, using all our resources of biblical, patristic and liturgical scholarship, and all the tools provided by phenomenology, psychology and philosophy. It must be seen from the viewpoint of Western man, not forgetting the contribution of the wisdom of the East and the experience of the non-Christian religions.

The *mystery of salvation:* a mystery in the twofold sense of a reality that is hidden, but also a reality that is now revealed and communicated to men in a history and through actual events.

The studies undertaken by the ecumenical institute at Jerusalem will revolve around this mystery. Professors of various denominations, with their researchers, will work together. This ecumenism that looks to the future in no way diminishes the importance of the ecumenical study engaged in retrospective analysis of the causes of our divisions. But this community of researchers and seekers will also be a "confessing" community. Here study and prayer will both have their part to play.[35]

A new mission is born in Jerusalem, seeking a new Judea, a new Samaria, to renew the uttermost parts of the earth.

[34] C. Moeller, *L'homme moderne devant le salut* (Paris, 1965).
[35] Cf. our article on the institute, in *Concilium* Vol. 17: *Historical Investigations* (Glen Rock, N.J.: Paulist Press, 1966).

Theodore Steeman, O.F.M./ *Den Haag, Netherlands*

Psychological and Sociological Aspects of Modern Atheism

I

How to Approach the Problem of Atheism Realistically

In dealing with atheism, as with any other religious problem, sociology and psychology concentrate on these phenomena as human realities, understood as arising from real people, individually or socially. The apparatus for this understanding is, therefore, borrowed from the reality of human life, individually or in society. Such a procedure implies that no stand is taken for or against belief in God. It is merely a matter of providing an intelligible presentation of belief and unbelief within the whole human sphere.

From this general observation about the method of the positive sciences of man, it follows that atheism can only be a problem insofar as it is one among other human religious phenomena. One may, however, say that atheism is a special problem insofar as it has but recently become a factor in human history and is still, at least from the ecclesiastical point of view, experienced as specifically problematic. But, from the point of view of the anthropological sciences, one has to accept that, in principle, belief is just as much a problem as unbelief, since normal situations are as full of problems as anomalous ones. Moreover, the deviation can only be seen as a genuine possibility when the normal

46

is no longer seen as self-evident and necessary, but precisely as the realization of a possibility of its own.

This means, therefore, that a psychological and sociological analysis is only possible within the wider framework of a more comprehensive analysis where belief and unbelief are treated on equal terms.

This does not mean that within this framework atheism has no specific features of its own. We should beware of glib conclusions. Just as the world of belief shows a rich variety of forms and content, so the world of unbelief is far from homogeneous. The prefixes "un" in unbelief and "a" in atheism already show that these phenomena are described in principle in a merely negative way. This can no doubt be justified. Formally atheism consists in the denial of God's existence. Beyond this the expression says practically nothing. It says nothing about what the atheist *does* believe in, how he lives or what values he accepts. It says merely that he does not believe in God. This purely negative description opposes him to the others, the people who believe in God. And so the believer is taken implicitly as the norm. The atheist is formally defined, or defines himself, by his denial of God's existence.

This is significant because, by the same token, atheism presupposes the world of belief in one form or another. The true atheist, the one who calls himself an atheist, is bound to have an idea of the God whose existence he denies. And when we call somebody an atheist, we can only do so insofar as we miss in the other the belief in God as we understand God. The dialogue about atheism is, therefore, primarily a dialogue about God or the belief in God. And it is by no means out of the question that the atheist tells the believer what kind of God he should believe in, namely, the God whom the atheist denies,[1] just as the believer

[1] Hamilton speaks here of the "Walter Kaufman syndrome": "Many secular modern atheists like their theological foes to be as orthodox as possible so they can be rejected as irrelevant (known as the Walter Kaufman syndrome, it has recently been repeated by secular critics of Bishop J. A. T. Robinson," in Altizer and W. Hamilton, *Radical theology and the Death of God* (New York, 1966), p. 6.

is sometimes inclined to tell the atheist that he is not really an unbeliever because the God he rejects is not God.[2]

With this the confusion is complete; for the moment it is obvious that there is no unequivocal definition of God, if such a definition were possible. Moreover, it is undeniable that the idea of God has developed and changed in the course of the centuries. The most recent development in the so-called radical theology[3] which starts from the "death of God" and so wants to pave the way for a Christian atheism makes the confusion still greater. No one still wants to call this group of theologians "atheists" in the traditional sense of those who deny God because they have arisen within the Christian Church itself. They carry too obviously the hallmark of faith.

A psychological or sociological investigation of the problem of belief or unbelief can, therefore, not start from a definition of God in its approach to belief or unbelief, in order to ask then under what conditions belief in such a God (from the human point of view) is possible and probable or impossible and improbable. Such a method would in any case narrow the field unjustifiably for the study of religious psychology and sociology. The variations of the idea of God are too important for anthropological sciences and, moreover, as psychologists and sociologists we are not entitled to make the genuineness of belief or unbelief depend on a particular definition of God or, more generally, on the object or content of faith.

[2] Mascall therefore thinks that he must protect the atheist, e.g., against Robinson because this author seems to say that "atheists are really unconscious crypto-theists". Mascall maintains that one should take the atheist seriously in his denial of God. "Most of them know quite well what belief in God is and, for reasons which seem to them quite convincing, reject it," in E. Mascall, *The Secularisation of Christianity* (London, 1965), p. 118. The difficulty is that Mascall, too, starts from a definite concept of God which he posits as the norm and which does not quite correspond to the concept of God which Robinson sees as being in suspense among both believers and atheists, and which he thinks he must reject.

[3] See, e.g., T. Altizer and W. Hamilton, *Radical Theology and the Death of God* (New York, 1966); W. Hamilton, *The New Essence of Christianity* (New York, 1966); P. van Buren, *The Secular Meaning of the Gospel* (New York, 1963).

How, then, can we tackle this? The only possible approach seems to be to begin with the religious life of man as a human reality and then to see what can be said about belief and unbelief, faith in God and atheism. This prompts the question of how to interpret these attitudes and convictions taken up by man.

II

MAN'S EXISTENTIAL WANT AND HIS RELATION TO GOD

I want to concentrate here on an element in modern religious philosophy because it seems to be of basic importance especially for the problem of atheism. In contrast with the obvious impossibility of reaching a satisfactory definition of religion by attempting a minimal or essential description of the object of faith, there is a tendency to define religion by one or other expression of human forces. Accordingly one reads then that religion is commitment to a great cause,[4] a central and dominant orientation of human activity,[5] a supreme dominant motive derived from a supreme value.[6] What kind of value this is in the concrete is not explicitly defined; it may be anything: God, science, the country, democracy,[7] and so on. What is essential in religion is rather looked for in the intensity, the coordinating power, the predominance of this value which gives life a concrete meaning and a sense of direction. Here we have an interesting inversion: while theology asserts that religious values are supreme and must be so, the other line maintains that the supreme concrete values are religious and must be recognized as such.

This tendency is so important because it complements in a

---

[4] J. Royce, *Sources of Religious Insight* (New York, 1912), pp. 199, 206 and elsewhere.

[5] W. Blackstone, *The Problems of Religious Knowledge* (Englewood Cliffs, New Jersey, 1963), p. 39.

[6] W. Christian, "Some Varieties of Religious Belief," in *Review of Metaphysics* 4 (1951), pp. 595-616; *idem, Meaning and Truth in Religion* (Princeton, 1966), pp. 60ff.

[7] Thus, for instance, P. Williams, *What Americans Believe and How They Worship* (New York, 1952), pp. 370ff.

valuable way our working notion of religion. The many attempts to find the psychological and human basis of belief in God usually end up with what is also presupposed in fact in the proofs for God's existence: in the wants of his existence man looks for a God that remedies this deficiency.[8] The deficiency of man and his world is, therefore, taken as the starting point, and God "fills the gaps".[9] God is, therefore, the ultimate cause or the fullness of being or the last refuge where the causality, the fullness of being or security are obviously inadequate within this world in order to make existence into a complete whole. This approach to the mystery of God is also wholly in agreement with man's search for totality, fullness and security.

Now, we can hardly accept that man's religious life can ever be explained without starting from man's existential dissatisfaction. To refer to a transcendental source of meaning, which must perforce contain the religious element, would not be explainable if we did not start from a lack of meaning in man's existence which is a primary fact. If human life is conceived as a closed existence, there is not much chance for a reference to a transcendence which would endow this existence with a meaning found in man himself, to be accepted by man.[10]

This existential want of man is easy to describe in more detail.

[8] G. Allport, *The Individual and His Religion* (London, 1951), pp. 137ff.; T. Luckmann, *Das Problem der Religion in der modernen Gesellschaft* (Freiburg i. Br., 1963), pp. 53ff.

[9] The expression comes from D. Bonhoeffer, *Widerstand und Ergebung. Briefe und Aufzeichnungen aus der Haft* (Munich, 1951).

[10] This holds also when one wants to put the origin of religion in religious experience. Religious experience must also be capable of being made intelligible as a human possibility starting from human existence itself, and then it points to the fact that in principle man is open to the sacred. If human existence were something closed in itself, religious experience would be impossible. It is, therefore, precisely here that the so-called projection theories find their limitation where religious life is concerned. The projection theory starts from human existence which is taken as something complete in itself; the religious expansion of existence is then understood as illusion, and religious experience itself as essentially an experience of man's self. The suggestion, made in this article, that the religious element may be localized more explicitly in the phenomenon of growth as part of human dynamics, may be seen as an attempt to indicate the limitation of the projection theory.

The most important fact of this want is probably death, but there are also the problems of illness, insecurity, natural disasters, guilt, loneliness, and so on. In many ways human life is a promise that is not fulfilled, a fullness that is negated.

But it is important to add, particularly with reference to a definition of religion in the expression of human forces, that the existential want of man is not necessarily experienced only as a lack, but also as a challenge to live in spite of all the disillusions of this life. A consequence of man's self-awareness is that he not only accepts this existence consciously but also becomes responsible for it. Human life is never a sheer process, not even a sheer conscious process, but also and always an act. Life must be lived and man must do this himself. Over against the wants and disappointments of life man has not only the possibility to complete his life and to turn it into a meaningful, livable whole, but also the very will-to-live, in spite of all the defects.

Here we touch upon a basic distinction which is important for that sound understanding of the human forces which lies at the root of religious life. Life itself shows already in its pre-conscious phases of development and in its process-like character the tension between completeness and openness, between integration and growth in new directions; and at the more conscious level we find that this continues in the tension between the search for security and the lure of adventure, between certainty and the urge for new experience. So we are forced to conclude that human life is not given as something finished but also as a field of possibilities that man must turn into reality. Life, therefore, if it is to be lived at all, must not merely be protected but also expanded. Along with that closed integrating system that ensures the human quality, there is that necessary openness with its opportunities for what is humanly possible. This is the basis for that open attitude toward the future that is of fundamental importance for man.[11]

If we want to apply this more directly to religious life we are

[11] This view is greatly inspired by Bergson's *Les deux sources de la morale et de la religion* (3rd ed., Paris, 1932).

faced here with two basic tendencies: the search for *security* in God and the religious motive in the stricter sense, the *commitment* to the cause of God. On the level of the notion we have about God, this distinction means: God as the answer to man's existential insecurity and God as the answer to the question why man should plunge into this insecurity; God as the final conclusion or God as driving force. The possibility of a notion of God who "fills the gaps" is, therefore, contrasted here with the possible notion of a God who summons man to a life that is meaningful and courageous, to love, to a God who brings all love to fulfillment (not in the sense of "completing" but as a challenge and a norm), and so provides the ultimate motives why man should accept the risk of living. God enters into life, not as one who solves the problems but rather as one who puts the problems to man. In another published study I distinguished two basic forms of faith on this basis, the *faith of trust* and the *faith of commitment*.[12]

I cannot develop this distinction here but I want to draw attention to its application to modern atheism. And I must add that both these forms of faith are in fact present in an adult attitude of faith in a vague kind of balance where the faith of trust is more or less the condition of the faith of commitment, and will lead to this faith of commitment unless it degenerates into a pathological self-centeredness. We may briefly summarize this relationship as follows: God is never merely the solution for man's problem; as soon as he is that, he becomes himself man's problem. In his existential want, man can long for God and then find his rest in God, but at that very moment he is charged with serving God.

[12] T. Steeman, *The Study of Atheism. A sociological approach* (Louvain, 1965), pp. 14ff.

III

The Change in the Attitude of Faith
and the Purification of the Notion of God

In the present context, however, it is more important not to concentrate on these two forms of faith in their ideal and fully developed combination but rather in their application to religious development. In general we must then say that trust and commitment or, if you like, the integration and growth, which underline them as dynamic needs, are dialectically related to each other. Growth becomes possible only when a certain integration has been achieved, and no integration can be so complete that growth is ousted. In that case the integration would suffocate. When the integrating tendency has reached a certain balance it will be interrupted by a new stage in growth. And if this is not to become an outgrowth which is beyond the possibility of being integrated in turn, it must be consolidated in a new phase of integration. But the growing process itself leads to an expansion of possible realization in the growing subject and allows it to be more and more itself. This process of human growth toward maturity shows a tendency to solve the problem of anxiety by strengthening self-confidence, and thus makes a more active and responsible life more possible.[13]

If we take, then, the situation of man's want as our starting point, we may say that the primary religious aspiration tends toward the source of meaning and security, which solves the problem of human insecurity. This is in line with the faith of trust and integration. It leads, however, to an attitude that is in principle a magical one, and this is important. What we experience as the solution for our existential want, remains, at least within the framework of the faith of trust, the sacred as ministering to man's insecurity. This holds already where magical ritual is credited with the power to force sacred powers, when man believes he has power over the sacred. One can trace this attitude further in

[13] See, for instance, E. Erikson, "The Healthy Personality," in *Identity and the Life Cycle* (Psychological Issues I, New York, 1959), pp. 61ff.

those forms of religiousness where the sacred, though forced, is seen as essentially a source of goodness and grace. In this perspective fall prayer of petition, prayer for forgiveness, a great deal of veneration of the saints. Whether these forms of religious activity may still be called magic is another question, and in a certain sense a question of definition; the basic motive, however, seems clearly to aim at a use of the sacred for man's own purposes. The sacred is then defined in function of man's experience of his want and so appears as that which rounds off man's existence so that it is fit for living.[14]

In contrast, the faith of commitment seems to push this human want into the background and the sacred becomes a value which is looked for and served for its own sake. And so the relatively rounded off completeness of existence, longed for and achieved in the faith of trust, is breached here, and the way is opened to a new definition of the sacred and the religious life. Therefore, we must look for the principle of development in religious life in this direction of openness toward the sacred. We find, then, within the scope of the faith of trust, the starting point for a religious renewal as well as the resistance provoked by this renewal. And at a later stage we shall find there the concrete result of what we acquired in religious growth.

In this light we can, in a very general way, discover a direction in the history of religion[15] which helps to understand the modern forms of atheism. We can establish a general recession of magic which goes hand in hand with a purification of the idea of God. More precisely, we find in the concrete religious systems a diminution of the practice of magic and a more spiritual understanding of the idea of God. Whether this same development is also

---

[14] For this distinction between magic and religion and the functional continuity between the primitive and the higher forms of religious behavior, see, above all, M. Weber, "Religionssoziologie," in *Wirtschaft und Gesellschaft* (Tübingen, 1922), pp. 246 and *passim*. Cf. T. Steeman, "Weber's Sociology of Religion," in *Sociological Analysis* 1 (1964), pp. 50-8. This is expanded in the study mentioned in footnote 12.

[15] Cf. the more specialized study by R. Bellar, "Religious Evolution," in *American Sociological Review* 29 (1964), pp. 358-74. Also, K. Hidding, *De evolutie van het godsdienstig bewustzijn* (Utrecht, 1965).

taking place in the field of religious motivation is as yet uncertain, but need not be considered here.

In any case, this much is clear: the development of a receding
magic and an increasing spiritualization of the idea of God seem
to belong to the process of a change in the experience of human
want. The coarser forms of magic are linked with the way in
which this existential want is experienced, that is, with the way
in which man's bodily existence is seen as insecure because of its
dependence on uncontrollable and ununderstood forces of nature.
The magic of rain is a good illustration. And without wishing to
simplify things here and to overlook the complicated psychical
and social processes which erect a concrete religious system on
the structure of want, it seems possible to establish a general
connection between the way in which concrete life is experienced as insecure and the forms of religious behavior arising in
such a situation. The purification of the idea of God must then
also be seen as dependent on the gradual increase in man's
control of natural processes or, at least, on his greater familiarity
with these processes. The rational control, even in still very
primitive symbolism, is just as much a presupposition for the
spiritualizing process in the concept of God as the reasoned
technical domination of nature, insofar as it changes the experience of man's existential want.

This process has essentially two aspects: on the one hand, man
is more conscious of himself, he asserts himself more powerfully
over against nature, within himself and outside, and as a result of
this rational control he achieves control over his own situation in
life; on the other hand, this indicates an interiorization process
that goes together with the purification of the idea of God. This
means that God is seen as less and less connected with natural
phenomena, and the sacred becomes more and more transcendental. Where nature and world lose in mystery, God, as *the*
mystery, is less looked for in the world.

But this implies a change in the balance between the faith
of trust and the faith of commitment insofar as these faiths
are expressed in concrete religious forms. In reality, the recession

of magic means at the same time an increase in the demand
and even the need for commitment. A God seen as less involved
in the world is at the same time a God who will be served. The
emphasis then shifts more toward moral responsibility, not as
a guarantee for God's blessing on harvest and fruitfulness but
as a value of its own, which demands faithfulness, even at the
cost of disadvantages or even life. God is then no longer so
much the giver of goods as he who summons man to moral
responsibility. In the same way, as man becomes materially
more independent and acquires control over his own situation,
the sacred is seen less in terms of concrete needs than in terms
of a challenge for life and for the right life. The faith of commitment becomes more important than the faith of trust.

IV

ATHEISM, THE DEMAND FOR OPENNESS
TOWARD THE GREATER GOD

At this point we may understand a little more about modern
atheism. We can now describe it as, for a large part, a protest
against a belief in God resting on man's inability to live this
life in a meaningful way. It is the God of the faith of trust that
has been declared dead, the God who has to supply the explanation for the situation of this world, the God who makes this
world appear better than it is, the God who fills the gaps and
covers up the shortcomings of human existence. In reality, behind
modern atheism lies what Bonhoeffer called the adulthood of
man,[16] man's awareness that in this life he has to create without
divine help and intervention, and whatever must become of this
world is his own responsibility. As a "standby", a final explanatory
hypothesis, a miracle worker, a last refuge, God disappears.
Man has become autonomous, is aware of his ability to explore,
control and know this world constantly better and more profoundly. For all this he does not need God, and he prefers to do

---

[16] D. Bonhoeffer, loc. cit., esp. the letter of April 30.

without a God who would merely explain the suffering of this world without abolishing it, and who would hamper his urge to find out and his efforts to improve life in this world. Modern man feels himself not really threatened any more, and where there is a real threat he wants to face it courageously, with a will to make this life more secure and with a manly acceptance of what happens to be man's lot: death, illness and weakness. God cannot take this weakness away or make it lighter. Man should be strong enough to accept this as part of his task in life.

This description is of course very general. In its concrete forms, atheism is not quite so homogeneous but, on the whole, we may see it in this light. It is an unquestionable fact that economic and technical development has placed man in a world so dominated by man that, on the whole, he feels much less the need to concentrate on the essential vicissitude of life. There is a kind of popular atheism which simply bypasses the question about the meaning of life and ignores the question of God more or less; in any case, it has little opportunity to pose the question at all. In a man-made world, the blame is now put on the fellow-man and one expects help from him. The most immediate existential needs must be met within the social and economic framework. The magic ritual is here replaced by the protest march, and there is no further room for any reference to a transcendental God.

But there are also great differences within the more consciously intelligent forms of atheism. For many, God's existence has become intellectually an incomprehensible affair, a superfluous hypothesis. For many others, it is morally impossible to believe in a God who tolerates bodily and moral suffering in this world. God may be good, but his world is certainly not, and if the world is not good, how then can one believe in a God who is? Others again get stranded in an intellectual *impasse* when the idea of God actually appears perhaps as no more than an escapist notion, a projection of man's dissatisfaction with the harsh realities that are, in fact, life; the assumption to let something exist as true because one would like it to be real although one never meets with it in reality. Sociological and psychological analyses of how concrete forms of faith are connected with certain cultural and psychological types were the red light for this group. Lastly, a number of motives for atheism arise as a protest against all the wickedness and injustice that has been caused by believers in the name of God.

These variations of the spectrum of atheism may add color but do not really affect the basic perspective. From what has been said we may at least conclude that modern atheism, both in its popular form and the more intellectual kind, shows what profound changes are taking place in the religious structure of humanity. As I said above, atheism cannot be detached from the image of God which it rejects, that is, from the dominant religious notions of Western culture. One can hardly pin down this image of God in a simple definition, but we may say that it is firmly entrenched in that form of faith that I called the faith of trust.[17] For Western man, God is still to a large degree the ultimate explanation, the last refuge, the conclusion of a philosophical argument, a terminus where one arrives when the road stops. According to the concrete formulations of the sacred, God becomes the sanction for the concrete ways in which the moral and social order are ordered as well as for the religious system that has been erected on this image-concept; and so he also becomes often enough a hindrance to social and economic progress. Where religious life is translated into concrete ideals, these, too, are very frequently set up as rigid ethical norms. Briefly, in spite of everything, we must admit that religious life in the West shows a high degree of closed finality at a time when man seems to be straining more than ever after a radical openness and responsibility, after a God who summons

---

[17] It is important to point out that the God who was declared dead by the radical theologians, is in fact the God of the faith of trust: "We trust the world, not God, to be our need fulfiller and problem solver, and God, if he is to be for us at all, must come in some other role," in W. Hamilton, op. cit., (n. 1), p. 40. Cf. H. Cox, The Secular City (3rd ed., New York, 1965), pp. 241ff.

him to a life of his own, rather than a God who tells him which way to go.

I am, therefore, inclined to see modern atheism, above all, as a turning away from the traditional approaches to the mystery that is God; as a criticism of what the general religious development has achieved so far. It is not yet clear whether a concept of God in terms of what I have called the faith of commitment can become culturally viable. But we may expect that God will become present again as the God who enjoins man to take his own task in life and his own responsibility seriously as a holy obligation.

Jules Girardi, S.D.B./*Rome, Italy*

Reflections on Religious Indifference

The doctrinal and "pastoral" [1] approach to atheism must be aware of the many forms it takes and must try to understand their original meaning. Here I want to put forward some reflections on one of them: religious indifference.

I

RELIGIOUS INDIFFERENCE AS A SPECIFIC FORM OF ATHEISM

This is the least conspicuous form of atheism; it has hardly any expression on the doctrinal level, and it rarely takes militant or aggressive forms on the practical level, so that one is tempted to pay less attention to it. However, it is of primary importance in the "pastoral" sphere. It represents, in fact, the most radical form of atheism; it challenges not only the existence of God and the possibility of knowing him, but the very consistency of the religious problem. Nowhere is the absence of God so total.

[1] We place "pastoral" in quotation marks. While using an accepted terminology, we feel we should point out the need to rethink its meaning when it is applied to relations with atheists, and more generally with all those who do not acknowledge the bishops and priests as their "pastors". The name and the thing ought perhaps to take account more clearly of the element of reciprocity which is present here.

What is more, religious indifference is often accompanied by indifference to any vision of the world and even to any ideal value. It is, therefore, the form of atheism which is least accessible to religious dialogue and, of course, to catechetical instruction. Dialogue presupposes, in fact, a common language, which is likely to be totally lacking when there is no meeting point even on the level of the problems. We cannot compare our answers when we do not even ask the same questions.

Indifference is an equally significant phenomenon because of its wide extent. The *Pastoral Constitution on the Church in the Modern World* states:

"In contrast to earlier times, to deny God or religion or to *ignore them* is no longer something unusual or likely to attract attention; it is often alleged to be demanded by scientific progress and a new kind of humanism. These trends are in many places no longer confined to the speculations of philosophers but very widely affect literature, the arts, the humanities, the interpretation of history and even civil law, so that many minds are disturbed" (n. 7). (*The italics are mine.*)

Indifference, then, is connected with certain major characteristics of modern civilization and thought, which I shall try to distinguish, and this connection both explains the wide extent of the phenomenon and reveals how deeply rooted it is.

Nor can we confine the phenomenon of indifference and the problems it raises to the psychological and sociological order; we shall see that it is related to a certain philosophical and theological image of religion, to which by that very fact it is a challenge.

Further, indifference does not affect only atheists in the strict sense; to a certain extent it affects all those for whom the religious problem is low in the order of their interests. It admits of several degrees, the highest of which is the absence of all religious concern, but in less marked forms it can penetrate the attitude even of believers.

Faced with an indifferent world, what should be the attitude of the Church? What can she say to one who ignores her? How can she try to renew herself so as to give a better response to the expectations of a world that expects nothing from her? How can she find new answers to old questions if the questions themselves have ceased?

I cannot possibly embark here on all these problems, though they are the most agonizing of our time. I wish simply to help toward posing them more precisely, by analyzing the nature and some of the causes of religious indifference.

II

PHENOMENOLOGY OF RELIGIOUS INDIFFERENCE

Enumerating the different forms of atheism, the *Pastoral Constitution on the Church in the Modern World* states in particular: "Others never even raise questions about God, since they never seem to feel any religious disquiet, or see why they should bother about religion" (n. 19). In the same context is a very similar position: "Some make so much of man that all vitality is taken out of faith in God—they seem more concerned to insist on man than to deny God." Later, speaking of systematic atheism, its justification is found in the thesis that man's autonomy is reckoned "incompatible with acknowledging the Lord, the author and end of all things—or at least they think *it makes such an acknowledgment superfluous*" (n. 20, *my italics*).

1. Origins and Dimensions

As a first approximation, then, religious indifference means that for a given person or milieu the religious problem does not even arise. God, whether he exists or not, is not a value, not something that counts. The question of his existence is purely "objective" and academic: it changes nothing in real existence. "God is dead" in the sense that he has ceased to be a value.

Religious indifference is, above all, a psychological attitude, a state of feeling, a mentality, an experience, within which the religious dimension finds no place. But this attitude comprises an attitude that is at least implicit, put into practice: a theory of religious indifference, the essential affirmation of which is that the question of God is simply not interesting. We shall see in a moment that such a theory can be the reflection of a whole interpretation of religion and life.

Religious indifference is not only a personal experience, it is also a social situation, the atmosphere of a milieu, in which everything—conversations, enterprises, projects, studies, decisions, legislation, etc.—happens as if the question of God did not exist. Personal and social indifference react on each other.

2. Practical Atheism and Religious Indifference

I have observed that religious indifference can affect the attitude even of theists. It is possible, in practice, to admit the existence of God as the existence of a reality in itself, of a "Supreme Being", a "First Cause", without this affecting real life. God is admitted as a Being, but not as a Value. He explains reality, but makes little difference to life. It is this Being who is sometimes called the "God of philosophy", in contrast with the "God of religion"; he is rather the God of *a certain* philosophy, one which is purely *objectivist*. The attitude of those who affirm the existence of God but live as if he did not exist, or who consider him to be a Being but not a Value, is often called "practical atheism".

Practical atheism and religious indifference are, therefore, two fairly similar attitudes; they have in common the idea that God is not a value, it makes little difference, it is of no importance whether one affirms or denies him. They are distinguished by the fact that the "indifferent" adopts no position on the theoretical issue, while the practical atheist theoretically affirms God's existence. But this theoretical difference has no "religious" bearing, and if we were to pursue the analysis further, we might, perhaps, question it even on the theoretical plane. Hence, we may conclude that the line of demarcation between theism and atheism is much less clear in practice than in theory, and that the problems raised by religious indifference may very largely concern theists.

3. *Discovery of the "Human Values"*

So far, I have described religious indifference from the negative point of view, which is what the term directly suggests. But a human attitude can never be sufficiently understood from the negative point of view; this can never be the central perspective. Here, as elsewhere, the first step must be the effort to understand, to look for the meaning. Now, one who is indifferent to religious values is not indifferent to all values; and we can only understand why he is indifferent to religious problems if we try to discover the values to which he is sensitive, which polarize his psychology, which people his "world".

There will always be secular, "lay", anthropocentric values. The "indifferent" man is too absorbed by human values to be interested in anything else. We have just read above that "some make so much of man that all vitality is taken out of faith in God—they seem more concerned to insist on man than to deny God" (n. 2).

These "human values" may, we suppose, be extremely varied. But the distinction between the eudaemonistic order and the moral order is supremely important. A man's interest may be purely selfish or else altruistic: the mere quest for immediate happiness or devotion to the service of a cause. In the first case, religious indifference signifies indifference to all ideal values. In the second, it goes with a certain "idealism", a certain secular "faith", which may be "communitary" and militant. In the first case, the explanation for the absence of feeling for religious values must be sought on a more general level: a man does not believe in religious values because ultimately he does not believe in anything. In the second, a man is uninterested in religious problems because he is absorbed by other ideal values: it is the presence of one faith that explains the absence of the other. The psychological and moral distance between religious faith and absolute indifference is much greater than between religious faith and secular "faith".

The affirmation of an ideal can be incorporated in an ideology (in the sense of a vision of the world), or it may be held as independent of any presupposition. In this case, it can be unconcerned with visions of the world or theoretical problems.

Religious indifference, then, sometimes stems from a disaffection to all visions of the world ("ideological indifference"); finally, it can be the expression of an even more radical attitude, the decline of all ideals ("absolute indifference").

III

ORIGIN AND EXPLANATION OF RELIGIOUS INDIFFERENCE

To attempt an explanation of religious indifference, we should have to answer two kinds of correlative questions: Why have secular values acquired a greater power of attraction? And why have religious problems ceased to interest a certain part of mankind?

The answer to the first order of questions would lead us first to examine, on the one hand, the many immediate attractions which "divert" (in Pascal's sense) the man of technical civilization, and, on the other hand, the awareness of the evil (in its individual, cosmic, economic, political, social, moral dimensions, etc.) which distresses him. The second order of questions would oblige us to examine the critical spirit, the pluralist atmosphere, the unification of the world, the sense of the historicity of truth and values, the autonomy of the values in relation to the ideologies, the existential inefficacy of religion, etc. It follows that religious indifference is not a superficial, passing expression, but the reflection of a situation that is worldwide, objective and subjective, a "sign of the time". It is not simply a personal attitude but an historical phenomenon of cosmic dimensions. Among the specific causes of religious indifference I shall here

consider only the existential inefficacy of religion and the autonomy of the secular values.

1. *The Deficiencies of the Christian Life*

The inefficacy seems to be at first a personal and social experience. Indifference, as an attitude of the person, is based
(explicitly or implicitly) on indifference as an objective situation:
belief or unbelief seems to make no difference to the reality of
things. Whatever one thinks of God, everything in fact happens
as if he did not exist. On the personal level, believers seem to be
men like others, or at least they are not so different from others
as to make one believe that faith has power to renew. On the
social level, the great religions, including Christianity, do not
seem to have transformed the world. The state of alienation
of persons, peoples and classes is more tragic today than ever;
the laws of political, economic and social life seem to be based
only on the principle of personal or collective self-interest, while
religion does not seem to be an historical force capable of in-
fluencing them. Has its most specific intervention in history—
which should be prayer, the recourse to providence—ever really
changed anything? Has it given history a new aspect? The scandal
of the "believers" is not chiefly that of some crime or other which
may have happened; it is, rather, the fact that nothing happens;
everything happens as if they were not there. There is no novelty
about Christianity; it does not startle the world.

2. *The Autonomy of the Secular Order*

But the inefficacy of Christianity is not considered as a question
of fact; it becomes more and more an assertion of principle
based on the autonomy of the secular order. The awareness of
that autonomy is based on awareness of the autonomy of man
himself, as end, author and norm of history. It seems that in
our day the role that God used to be called on to play in our
world is filled by man in a more sure and efficient way. The
explanation of natural and historical phenomena is provided
by science, for which God is an unnecessary hypothesis. The

scientific explanation more effectively takes the place of the occult causes and the *deus ex machina* of former times. The transformation of nature and society, for which men formerly trusted in divine providence, is provided by technology and social action. The power of technology, organization and solidarity likewise responds to that need for security which was once sought in God.

In the same way, secular institutions are conscious of their autonomy in relation to religious institutions (for example, the State in relation to the Church). They are emerging from that tutelage and so are coming of age. In the modern world, secular institutions, admitting no foundation but the dignity of man, fulfill more surely and efficiently the tasks formerly entrusted to religious institutions. Moreover, religion, by proclaiming that it transcends the secular order and is "indifferent" toward particular regimes, would seem to authorize men to erect into a principle its inefficacy in the secular sphere. If religion is indifferent toward the organization of the world, it is surely natural for the world to be indifferent toward religion. On a deeper level, if God is habitually silent in history, is it surprising that man does not listen to him?

On the subjective level, reductionist psychology provides a similar interpretation of man's conscious life and gives religious indifference its immediate basis. Religion does not correspond to any specific need; it can be explained as the extrapolation of frustrated earthly desires. The secularization of the moral conscience is here particularly significant. Morality based on the extrinsic intervention of God, appears to be a provisional and infantile stage.

Under these conditions, religion does not seem to be capable of producing new men, still less, a new human race.

Indifference, then, exists implicitly or explicitly in relation to a certain image of religion, on which it makes a critical judgment concerning its value rather than its truth.

Thus, we can understand, in relation to indifference, the meaning of the Council's text on the origin of atheism: "Atheism, fully considered, is not something spontaneous or fundamental, but the result of various causes among which we must list critical reaction against religion, which in some places means chiefly against the Christian religion" (*Pastoral Constitution on the Church in the Modern World*, n. 19).

IV

THE CHURCH FACED WITH GRAVE DECISIONS

From these reflections we can see how vast are the problems raised by indifference, problems that affect all relations between Christianity and the modern world. The most dramatic aspect of the contemporary situation is not the decline of the old solutions but the decline of the problems themselves. The atheism of the future seems to be tending toward those peaceable and untroubled forms rather than to committed and militant denials.

The difficulties of the dialogue, which I have noted above, can now be seen in all their gravity. On the one hand, dialogue on the religious plane does not interest the world of indifference. On the other hand, can the Church as such accept a dialogue on the ground of mere humanization and agree to play down her mission of evangelization? Would she not thus risk becoming a philanthropic institution, making herself worldly in order to be accepted by the world? The dilemma can be agonizing for the Christian conscience: either to engage in a dialogue of the secular order and abandon her true mission, or else to stick to her mission, but lose contact with large masses who seem to be inaccessible to the religious message.

Insofar as indifference exists in relation to a certain image of Christianity that no longer makes any impression on men today, it raises the problem of the genuineness of that image and stresses the need for a profound rethinking of Christianity, in view of the new situation, above all, as to what concerns the "presence" of God. This attitude of honest research is, moreover, one of the marks of the conciliar Church, and it is notably expressed on the subject of atheism. The Church "is aware of the seriousness of the questions raised by atheism, and out of charity toward all men she believes that those questions should be deeply and seriously examined" (*Pastoral Constitution on the Church in the Modern World,* n. 21).

Further, this set of problems, precisely because of its many historical connections, is even wider than Christianity, and concerns all the religions, the ideologies, the "faiths". It is, in short, the problem of the meaning of our age that is thus forcibly presented to the conscience of the whole world.

Karl Rahner, S.J./*Munich, West Germany*

In Search of a Short Formula of the Christian Faith

How Intelligible Is the Christian Message Today?

If the Church wants her mission to be effective in the situation of modern unbelief, she must be able to express the Christian message in such a way that it becomes really intelligible for modern man. This truism, however, demands something very difficult and very often dealt with in an unsatisfactory manner. For the message must be expressed in such a way that the essential stands out clearly from everything secondary and can in fact be "realized". Otherwise a modern "pagan" cannot distinguish this essence of Christianity from the often not very inviting and even repellent outward "image" of the Church (in preaching, religious practice, social relationships, etc.), and he will then extend to Christianity itself his partly justified objection to Christians. This formula must be able to state the essentials briefly for the busy man of today in a way that can be repeated again and again. Such repetition will not become tedious when it really gives what is essential and decisive so that man does not see it merely as a kind of "ideology" which meets him from "outside" and does not affect the "facts of life", but rather as the reality of his own life, such as he experiences and undergoes it.[1]

[1] This will not strike us as some kind of modernism when we remember that the outward preaching of the Gospel is always already forestalled by the grace of Christ.

The need for such a "short formula" is particularly pressing in our *pluralistic* society. In earlier days a homogeneous society could, as a whole, "live" this Christianity at least as a "religion" though perhaps not always as a "personal faith". In a situation where man was already imbued with Christianity as a social habit and an ideology, even *before* he was capable of, and forced to, a personal decision in faith, Christianity could be doctrinally transmitted with a minimum of worry. This could later on apply to some extent not only to baptism but also to life itself. There was no need to be so careful about the correct proportions of the terms of the statement; one could put forward what was only of secondary importance as more urgent than what was of primary importance; one might even neglect that *one wholeness* of Christianity, as such, which is today precisely the condition for any true understanding and realization of any particular statement contained therein. Today, however, the baptized Christian, particularly if born in a Christian family, has to live in an existential situation which, in itself, by no means communicates Christianity. Insofar as his situation is concerned, even a baptized person is to a large extent more "pagan" than the pagans in the days of Constantine. He must have a sufficiently clear understanding of what is proper to, and truly distinctive of, Christianity to discover his Christian identity in his environment.

The Structure of Such a "Short Formula"

When one ponders on these various needs, one is surprised that there are so few "short formulas" that express the real essence of the Christian message briefly and in a way that can be understood today. "Short" must be taken here, of course, in a very relative sense. It need not be as brief as the Apostles' Creed or some similar official confession of faith. On the other hand, a kind of modern "small catechism" would be far too long and would, moreover, not really suit what I mean here for other reasons. Nor is it necessary to find a formula suitable for all countries and for all manner of culturally and socially different groups of human beings. It would also be much more short-lived in our constantly and rapidly changing world than, for instance, the Apostles' Creed. Therefore, it is more necessary to have such formulas for mind, heart and memory. They must be assimilable both immediately and "existentially", self-explanatory and not be in need of a long preliminary explanation before they can persuade; formulas that speak to modern man immediately within his own sphere of thought and from his own experience. They must, as far as possible, use the contemporary vocabulary and make use of such presuppositions as are self-evident to modern man, regardless of whether in themselves they are more so than others or not. They should not take for granted as evident what is precisely not evident in such a way that it can be understood and basically experienced as such without further ado. These requirements for such a short formula are frankly not quite as clear and evident as one might think.

Let me illustrate this with a simple example. One would suppose that all short formulas of the faith,[2] from the New Testament on, assume that the listener has the right understanding of the word "God", and that this understanding can easily become existentially real to him. But is that so today? Can we still say today with St. Thomas that the phrase *Quid est Deus* (what is God) is clear to *all* and known by *all,* and that, therefore, the question is at most whether this particular "God" exists? Today, things are not really quite so simple.[3] Nor is it enough to produce a definition, however clear and glibly spelled out, of "what" is *meant* by this word. Should such a short formula not start today at a point far beyond this, where one experiences in one's own existence what is really meant by "God"? But where do we find the starting point for such a

---

[2] One might already see such a short formula in the "decalogue" of the Old Testament since it should be understood as the formulation of a covenant rather than as the codification of norms of morality or natural law.

[3] For this, see K. Rahner, "Bemerkungen zur Gotteslehre in der katholischen Dogmatik," in *Catholica* 20 (1966), pp. 1-18.

contemporary understanding of the meaning of the word "God" and for the existential expression of it? And what kind of starting point could really and explicitly put this into words, and that briefly?

These simple considerations already show how far the themes and proportions of such a contemporary formula would have to differ from those of the past. Above all, we should have to see what character such a short formula should assume to suit a situation where, for the first time in history, genuine atheism plays a decisive role. The same concern should apply to the *christological* statements in such a formula. These christological statements should, from the very start, be formulated in such a way that they do not sound like a myth from antiquity rooted in a past where, for modern man, it is no longer possible to find out *what* exactly happened at that time. For him such a past could certainly no longer be relevant for this age.

About the History of the "Short Formulas"

Before attempting to compose such a short formula, which is meant to be no more than an experiment,[4] I still have something to say in order to make such a formula better understood. I only mention here a *requirement* that must be filled by both dogmatic and pastoral theology as well as by actual preaching in this age of a pluralistic society and of atheism. What follows is meant to strengthen this requirement.

The history of these "short formulas" is as old as Christianity itself. Already in the New Testament the statement that "Jesus is the Messiah" (cf. e.g., Acts 9, 22 and John 20, 31) constituted for the Jew, who still lived in the environment of Old Testament Judaism, a formula that said practically everything he had to know and to confess to be a Christian. It was a formula that was basically and directly intelligible to him.[5] Romans

[4] In the second part I am offering an enlarged form of an earlier attempt; cf. K. Rahner, "Kurzer Inbegriff des christlichen Glaubens für 'Ungläubige'," in *Geist und Leben* 38 (1965), pp. 374-9.

[5] For a more detailed study of these early confessions of faith in the New Testament, see K. Lehmann, *Auferstanden am dritten Tag* (Freiburg, 1967).

10, 9 (Jesus as the risen Lord) is another similar formula that expressed clearly and distinctly the minimum of Christian belief in its essence for a "theist" of those days. If one understood and accepted what was thus expressed, then one was certainly a Christian in those days. 1 Thessalonians 1, 9 would provide such a formula for the Gentile type of Christian. And if one wished to study these short formulas in patristic history, a large part of it (though not the whole) would be occupied by the "symbols of the faith", the creeds; and here one should notice that, apart from the official ecclesiastical creeds in the stricter sense, there also was always a more "private" kind of formula (such as that of bishops when they assumed office, etc.). One might also include here such small writings as Augustine's *Enchiridion,* in spite of their wider scope (*P.L.* 40, pp. 181-196). Such a formula is, for instance, also Luther's pungent paraphrase of the Apostles' Creed in his *Small Catechism.*

The most recent attempt at—or rather, demand for—such a short formula, in one sentence, is contained in Vatican II's *Decree on the Missionary Activity of the Church.* In the elementary situation in which the baptized person finds himself, the believer must understand that in Christianity "he is saved from sin and introduced into the mystery of God's love which is communicated to him in Christ" (n. 13). Although such a short sentence does not yet by itself constitute a formula, it contains, nevertheless, a demand for it and gives some indications toward it. Such a sentence clearly is not afraid of an "anthropological" perspective of the creedal statement. It gives the substance of the faith as a statement made by man, and for him it is God's self-communication in which he understands what he is and what God is.

The Urgency of This Task for Theology

Public life today is filled with propaganda slogans, party programs and manifestos by which social groups want to convey to everyone else what they are and what they stand for. Such statements are prepared with extreme care. They cannot be replaced by fat volumes or a series of conferences, yet, must contain all the necessary essential points in such a way that they can effectively be put across to the masses in a pluralistic society. Something similar is required for the Church's preaching in the age of atheism.[6] Such a brief formula of the Christian message, of which we need so many today, cannot be found in the old creeds, even though these remain the "rule of faith". Perhaps dogmatic theology and catechesis will tackle this soon if the need for it is recognized. It is not merely a matter of religious education, but also a matter of dogma, and hence, of philosophy and culture. To achieve the right kind of statement of faith in God is a matter that extends far beyond the problem of religious education.[7]

A Suggested Brief Formula of the Christian Faith

In what follows I have attempted to draft such a "modern" confession of faith. It is really not more than an attempt, the emphases can be distributed differently, and it can be lengthened or shortened. Obviously it will be understood only by educated Westerners, if at all. But this seems to me no objection in itself. Otherwise it might become so suitable for everybody that it is not really suitable for anybody in particular. Did not the old creed itself become "generally intelligible" as a traditional and sacred formula because it was first of all adequate only for a very small cultural group? And if someone says that he cannot do anything with this attempt, no one will indeed reproach him for this, on condition that he himself knows better how one should make plain to a contemporary "unbeliever" in his own environment *what* we Christians really believe, and how to put this briefly. Would it not be useful if the new Roman Secretariat for Unbelievers someday produced such examples of a very short

[6] That such a form of religious "propaganda" is inseparably linked with the specifically intimate element of personal faith needs no special elucidation. For a more extensive treatment see K. Rahner, in *Handbuch der Pastoraltheologie*, ed. by F. X. Arnold, K. Rahner, V. Schurr, and L. M. Weber, vol. II/1 (Freiburg, 1966), pp. 146-51.

[7] For the historically different approach to faith, see K. Rahner, in *Handbuch der Pastoraltheologie* II/1, pp. 142ff.

catechism? Such examples should follow the line of the *Decree on Ecumenism* which lays down that there is a very important distinction between the "foundations" of the faith and other truths. They should establish the value of the old formulas not by simply repeating them but by putting them into a new light. And should a doubtless necessary explanation (recognized as legitimate and necessary even by the strictest defenders of the lasting validity of the old formulas) always be so much longer than the old formulas themselves? If not, then the apologist of the old formula should also be able to produce a brief "confession of faith" that expresses the old, enduring truth but expresses it differently from the traditional formulas. As I said before, it is in this sense that I should like the following attempt to be understood. It is only presented in the hope that it will soon be followed by more and better ones.

In his spiritual existence, man will always fall back on a sacred mystery as the very ground of his being, whether he admits this explicitly or not, whether he lets this truth come through or tries to suppress it. This mystery, which permanently contains and sustains the small circle of our knowing and doing in our daily experience, our perception of reality and our free activity, as an ineffable and therefore not articulated circumference, lies at the very root of our being; it is self-evident but, by the same token, most hidden and unheeded; it speaks in its silence and is present in its absence while it shows us our limitations. We call this God. We may overlook him, but even when in our action we show ourselves uninterested in him, he is still affirmed as the ground on which this action rests, in the way in which a logical argument is still operative in an action that denies its validity; or in the way in which a statement about the absolute meaninglessness of all is considered more meaningful than the acceptance of a meaning to existence: such an explicit statement affirms once again "meaning" as the ground of reality. As the ground of the individual's existence, involved in perception and action, the sacred mystery that we call God is most deeply within us and at the same time so far beyond us that it does not need us. Reverence and worship befit him. Where these are present, where man accepts his existence in full responsibility, where man seeks and expects his ultimate meaning trustingly, there he has already found God by whatever name he may call him, since his ultimate name can forever be spoken only in a love that is speechless before his incomprehensibility.

However hard and uncertain it may be for us to interpret this deepest and totally primordial experience in the ground of our being, man nevertheless experiences in his most inward development that this silent, infinitely distant, sacred mystery, always pointing to the limitations of his finite being and revealing his guilt, allows him nevertheless to approach it; it enfolds him in an ultimate and radical love that meets him as salvation and as the real meaning of his existence as long as he allows the possibilities of this love to be wider than his own limitation and guilt.

This love, experienced in the ground of our being, is nothing else than God's absolute self-communication in which God gives himself (and not merely something finite) and in which the infinitely distant becomes the circumference of our existence; and it is this we call deifying grace. It is offered to all as light and as the promise of eternal life; it works freely and graciously in every man from the primordial source of his existence. And so it appears, even though nameless, wherever in man's history courage, love, faithfulness to one's conscience, endurance in darkness through belief in light or the recognition of the ground of one's being as the sacred mystery of God's loving nearness— wherever all this is at work or comes to light.

Insofar as history allows God's pledge of himself, accepted in faith, hope and love, and in his radical self-communication to man, to break through with increasing clarity, we speak of history of salvation and revelation. This is the shape of the historical "category" in which God's "transcendental" self-communication, given from the beginning in the ground of man's being (in virtue of that deification of man which it effectuates through grace), becomes constantly more manifest. It is true that this process is often thwarted and obscured through the history of that guilt incurred by man when, in the mystery of his refusal, he locks out God's grace and limits himself to an exclusively self-centered understanding. Yet, the process is at work everywhere and always because the mystery of the God who reveals and communicates himself in love is more powerful than the mystery of human guilt.

This history of man's self-discovery in the ground of his deified being (a deification which is at least present as an "offer"), the history of this tangible self-discovery in God in time and space (always in virtue of that divine promise we call grace), reaches its historical climax and the final goal which in a hidden way carries this whole historical process, in him whom we simply call the God-Man in this deified humanity. All seek him, not explicitly, yet really, whenever they desire that the ultimate experience of the radical meaning of their being, of their being subject to death and of God's ultimate acceptance become manifest in their history, and thus wholly present and finally confirmed. To this degree, insofar as we are concerned, every man who is faithful to his conscience is an "Advent" Christian, a Christian who looks forward to the *one* man in whom the real issue (which we actually *are* and do not simply think up arbitrarily) and God's pledge have become one in one person and so have become manifest as ultimately valid. As Christians we have the courage to believe that what is here sought, has been found. It is Jesus of Nazareth.

He who has experienced God in Christ in this way, will and must confess him. He does this not as if those who cannot yet recognize the fulfillment of their hidden experience by name, are excluded from God's mercy in which he gives himself to us insofar as we do not deny him. It is, rather, that he who has found Christ must confess him before his brethren. This means, in the first place, simply that he accepts both life and death, such as they are, in obedience. In doing so he meets Christ. It means further that we constantly renew our acceptance of God's forgiveness when we look on him and, finally, that we explicitly confess his name and thus confess the hope we find in him.

Christ is he in whom God's self-communication and man's acceptance of it have become one in existential reality through the act of God; in whom God himself is present in the highest degree and irrevocably *there* where we are; and in whom man has become the manifestation of God himself not only as a demand for God but also as God's pledge. Christ is the son of man quite simply and the Son of God in the unconditional truth of this Word. That the goal of salvation history, which carries this salvation history, fulfills it and irrevocably ensures its victory over the history of death, has become an historical, concrete fact in Jesus of Nazareth is recognized by the Christian in faith. Mankind, throughout its history, seeks the God-Man as the fulfillment of its own salvation history; it has found no one in whom it can recognize this God-Man except Jesus of Nazareth. In the excellence of his life, in his death and resurrection, he shows himself as this God-Man, as the presence of God himself in mankind's history. In him God is once and for all he who has accepted us in love and whose fullness of truth, life and eternity has become our own possession. The Christian believes in the death of Jesus in which mankind has yielded its own "ground" and purpose to God's grace, and in the perfect fulfillment of the man Jesus, called his resurrection, in which mankind has already begun in a direct manner to possess the life of God himself, thereby surpassing its history in time and space.

Insofar as God remains forever the sacred incomprehensible mystery in his self-communication, sharing his divinity without losing it, we call him Father. Insofar as God communicates himself to us as our most intimate and eternally valid life through his deifying grace in the ground of our being, we call him Holy Spirit. Insofar as he appears historically in the God-Man as the real truth of our existence, we call him the Word of God and the Son of God. Insofar as both these ways of God's self-communication, which mutually support and condition each other, really communicate God himself, and not a merely creaturely and finite representation of God, we confess that God, while in himself and in his own being he remains one, is distinguishably Father, Word and Spirit, so that we call him triune, Father, Son and Spirit, one God.

The community of those gathered around Jesus in faith, who expect to share in his fulfillment in hope and in him are linked with the Father and one another through his Spirit in love, is what we call the Church. He himself founded this Church in his first disciples and gave it a constitution in the twelve messengers whom he entrusted with his mission, endowed with his Spirit and united in Peter as head of this college of apostles; these twelve were authorized to pass on this constitution with their office. He gave this Church the task and the authority to represent him and to bear witness to him in history until the end so that he would remain and be operative in constantly new ways within the concrete process of history as the pledge of God's self-communication. Derived from Christ in its origin and witness, the Church is, therefore, the historical sign of God's victorious will to save, which overcomes all human guilt. In this sense the Church is the "sacrament" (i.e., the sacred and effective sign) through which the deification of the world becomes manifest and in this manifestation becomes effective. As the historical presence of God's self-promise in Christ, the Church's confession is found there where it is expressed in the definitive witness of its teaching office and prevents a falling away from God's truth. The Word by which the Church transmits, by means of sacred symbols, the grace alive in it for its own fulfillment to the individual believer for the decisive moments of his own situation in life, is an effective Word which brings along with it what it signifies. This Word, therefore, is itself a sacrament.

Just as in his personal existence man is aware of words that commit him completely and that show what happens in the very fact of being pronounced—for example, words of ultimate love or of forgiveness—so the Church possesses words in which it offers man precisely what it is, namely, a sign of God's mercy and God's love for all.

The Church knows seven such words of grace: the sign of grace (called baptism) in which, through ritual ablution, the sinful man dedicates himself to the triune God and is accepted as a member of the Church in the concrete process of history (through forgiveness of guilt and sanctification by the Spirit of God); the word in which the explicit promise of the Spirit is linked with a laying on of hands (confirmation), and which empowers the baptized Christian to testify to God's love of the world through witness and his own life, also with regard to those that think they cannot believe in his love; the corrective and forgiving word (confession) by which the Church reconciles a guilty member to herself and to God; the word in which the Church, with a ritual unction, commends the baptized Christian in his agony to the God of eternal life (last anointing); the word, linked with a laying on of hands, by which the Church grants one of its members, in three different stages, a share in its office and the power to exercise its function (ordination); the word that confirms the marital bond (sacrament of marriage) and makes it the image of the fruitful union in love between God and that humanity gathered in the Church in Christ. To these six signs of sanctifying grace must be added a seventh which is the supreme one: the sacred meal of Christ's community where this community commemorates its salvation in the death and resurrection of its Lord and constantly renews its union with its Lord in a ritual meal under the signs of bread and wine: the sacrament of the eucharist. And so, the Church is at the same time the visible community of the redeemed and the sign under which God's Spirit works the salvation of the world and shows it forth in a visible manner.

Insofar as the Christian is united with his Lord through his Spirit in faith, hope and love, he knows that he is already freed from all worldly power and forces (sin, law and death) and on his way to a share in the infinite and ultimate validity of the life of the true and living God. But he also knows that he must share with his Lord the fate of death where he, too, must surrender his existence in the hands of the living God, and where his life and death seem to be an utter abandonment by God and the ultimate darkness of guilt. He knows that his life must be the active expression of an unconditional love of God and his fellow-man, a love that is the overriding fulfillment of all law. He is consoled by the hope that when his own life and the history of mankind draw to an end, all others, the loved ones, will see in unveiled fulfillment what has already been given in faith and humility, namely, the life of God who is all in all.

Karl Lehmann / *Munich, West Germany*

Some Ideas from Pastoral Theology on the Proclamation of the Christian Message to Present-Day Unbelievers

All bloodless, abstract ideas are dangerous when formulated schematically. Many of them already constitute a signal for uninhibited attacks on the "opponent" as "insects" or "vermin". Because the unbeliever generally speaks of the "theist" and the believer speaks of the "atheist" from a similarly abstract distance, this kind of encounter all too easily degenerates into shadow-boxing, in which neither partner has really ever properly seen the other.

This confusion cannot be dispelled within the space of a short article.[1] Let us just raise three questions: In what way is a meaningful approach to the modern unbeliever theologically and pastorally possible? What are the necessary basic structures for the concrete kerygma? What principles of public Church action are particularly urgent today concerning life with unbelievers and to the missionary task of the Church?

[1] In the following there are, intentionally, very few references to the literature and to the testimonies of atheism, in accordance with the particular nature of this volume on pastoral theology. In order to fill out the picture, perhaps the author may refer the reader to his essay "Die Auseinandersetzung mit dem westlichen Atheismus und der pluralistischen Gesellschaft: *Die Zukunft der Kirche,* ed. by O. Mauer (Vienna and Freiburg: Herder Verlag, 1967). Here the author pursues ideas that come partly from the theology of K. Rahner, as expressed, in particular, in his *Handbuch der Pastoraltheologie,* Vol. II/1-2 (Freiburg, 1966). Here an exemplary application of these ideas to the problem of atheism is attempted. I refer the reader to this work for fuller analyses and bibliographies.

I

THE APPROACH TO UNBELIEF AS A PROBLEM

In everyday life even the external coming-together of men who hold totally different views is a difficult situation and potentially productive of much conflict. This grows even more acute when it is a question of philosophies of life (ideology) and of religion. The most important thing is to remain aware of the different forms of the phenomenon of "atheism".

The Nature and Different Varieties of Contemporary Atheism

There are very many kinds of "atheists": the man who is anti-clerical, superstitious, anti-institutional, morally and intellectually blunted or primitive, the "non-practicing" Christian, the man who has fallen away secretly in his heart, the unbeliever from childhood, the sectarian, the skeptic on principle, etc. But these are only labels. However valuable the knowledge of typologies, pastoral theology must at the same time take account of the variety and uniqueness of the different types. Umbrella terms can only do damage. For example, a "mature atheist", M. Machovec, is himself ashamed of some of the forms of anti-religious atheism that do not seem any less terrible, inhuman and backward to him than to us. On the contrary, we should perhaps call someone an "unbeliever" who observes and follows with great regularity, in an exterior way, an empty liturgical ceremonial and, while belonging (sociologically of course) to a Church society, has no concern in his concrete life for the presence of the *living* God. The honesty of human, and certainly of religious, dialogue leaves only one approach to the secret or open sources of atheism: the real suffering from which this lack of belief springs.

But it is a particular characteristic of modern unbelief that it does not acknowledge such "suffering" and the necessary pointer it contains toward something like "salvation", "redemption" or "bliss". The "troubled atheist", as Karl Rahner calls him, is a rare case. Such a man does not deny God outright, but suffers—soberly, bitterly or desperately—from the absence and the intangibility of God and from the torturing mysteriousness of alienated existence. That is why he experiences this Godless world and its activity as dead, fragmentary, questionable, ambiguous and mysterious. The more radical forms of unbelief today also negate the basic assumption of such sufferings: they dismiss the idea that the world could be different or that "another" significance could appear. The attempt at *any kind of* "transcendence" is denied. We are here in the world, and it is only a question of accepting it critically in its brutality, in the engagement of one's freedom in relation to it and (perhaps) of changing it or of living as one pleases without inhibitions. "Objectivity" is the only law. But here also are the most varied ways of behavior. There is the sheerest indifference as the only answer to hopelessness and the "absurd" dependence of the world on chance; a constant heroic struggle to change the world; aggressive polemic against all veiling of our disastrous situation and against any attempt at comfort.

The prototype of today's unbeliever is not simply to be found in the New Testament: the hard-hearted Jew who is zealous for the law of God, but does not follow God's own ways; the proud Greek, who seeks for a timeless general truth of ideas, and can see salvation on the cross only as "folly". Unbelief is undoubtedly the result of all the unmasking of ideological phenomena in religion and the Church, but today it is not very often polemical. It has finished with all that; it has become indifferent. It is "experienced" because it has done away with the magic of everything in heaven and on earth. It willingly accepts the pain of this sobering realization, as it does not seek to explain the mystery of the world by "metaphysical hypotheses" or "transcendent stopgaps", but reminds finite man, foiled with the superior odds of reality, of his own unique responsibility. Such a life is impressive: this concrete, spontaneous and adaptive relation to the world with its incomparable sense of reality makes the "bourgeois" world's patterns of thought and behavior seem a hollow system of lies and ideologies;[2] it regards itself in all the full intensity of existence as the successful life that refuses to deliver man by some utopian philosophy into the hands of foreign powers. It frequently appears as the image of a highly qualified "hero", to whom one could apply the words "virtue" or "sanctity", if these had not been removed from one's vocabulary.

But this is not necessarily the last word. The life that is no longer experienced as held in the tension of something greater, can certainly "go on", but it leads to nothing; it simply breaks off or else ends in a desert of the banal. The indifference we have described does not merely destroy the idea that man could ever reach a saving origin, but also the illusion that the vain search will ever end. In this way the claim to truth becomes all the more intense, the more clearly it is seen as unquenchable. The more acutely the "death of God"[3] is experienced, the more threatening does the question of his presence become. The marginal doubt may appear as to whether we have really finished with God.

The Methodological Starting Point

One should not simply take the terrifying variety of these limited situations, place them immediately in a Christian context and seek to see latent Christianity in all and everything. These bastions too must perhaps be given up if the dialogue with the "unbelievers" is to be successful. Nowhere do we see the embarrassment that then arises more clearly than in the question of the right concrete methodological starting point and way of preach-

[2] The problems of ideology and Christianity, insofar as pastoral theology is concerned, are here excluded. Cf. *Handbuch der Pastoraltheologie* II/2 (Freiburg, 1966), pp. 109-202.

[3] The range of questions connected with this phrase would require special historical and analytical treatment in order to work out the real doubt that lies in this idea of the "death of God". The frivolity of "theologians after the death of God" (in terms of the history of ideas and of the fact itself) misses the seriousness of the situation, although they pride themselves on the opposite. The same thing is true of talk about the "end of metaphysics". Here we desire only to point to the absolute need for extensive and very subtle investigation of these things.

ing to unbelievers. From the beginning there is so much "strangeness" between the fronts that any direct approach seems problematical. Nor does a "theology of unbelief" help very much, if it means that, together with other "theologies" (of lay apostolate, etc.) there is another further field where specialists can busy themselves. Even if this attempt is concentrated on the idea of "dialogue", this direct approach is problematic because neither the capacity for faith to engage in dialogue is automatic nor is it certain that unbelief can be approached in dialogue.[4] The situation of dialogue is given only insofar as the general intellectual, sociological and political situation of man brings about a situation of mutual influence that precedes any reflective act or personal decision. As long as atheism shows only defiance, indifference or silence in relation to faith, and as long as sectarian importunity, tactless propaganda and enlisting the aid of secular forces in favor of the Christian "faith" are today completely out of the question, there remains only one possibility for the kerygma and theological work in relation to unbelief:[5] theology and kerygma today must be, from the very beginning and in everything they do, a theology and kerygma *for* "pagans", irrespective of whom they are addressed to. If kerygma is conceived as something "apart" from various other things that must now *also* be pursued with pastoral zeal, if "theology for unbelievers" will become a new specialized discipline with all kinds of external borrowings from everywhere, then it will profoundly mistake its task.

We shall describe this methodological principle in a little more detail:

1. Only a theology and kerygma that accept and share distress of contemporary man with his—perhaps wrongly interpreted— experience of the "distant and dead" God, can express the word

---

[4] Cf. E. Biser, "Dialog mit dem Unglauben. Möglichkeiten und Grenzen," in *Wort und Wahrheit* 21 (1966), pp. 339-47.

[5] For this idea cf. also what K. Rahner says in "Die Herausforderung der Theologie durch das Zweite Vatikanische Konzil" which appears in the compendium mentioned in footnote 1.

of salvation in a new language in such a way that the unchange-
able Gospel of Christ can be understood without the necessity
for defensive skirmishes or dispensing with large parts of it.

2. Only because the true believer knows that he has within
him a possible latent "no" to the grace of God, is he able, when
faced with this real and, in this life, irremovable suffering, to
express himself to some extent concerning the doubts and problems of unbelief. Since the Christian himself is living in the same
general intellectual situation, he shares in the sufferings of the
world around him, however different his life in faith might be.

3. Only in the free acceptance of the difficulties that arise
from contemporaneous mental co-existence and in the frank acknowledgment of the constant threat to one's own faith—including all the most conscientious scientific reflection about this basic
situation that is inseparable from faith—do we find the key to the
intellectual and spiritual honesty that alone gives a reliable basis
on which there could be a possible offer to the unbeliever and a
real "dialogue". Such a "confession of faith" is as far from an
imagined security—that fears *any* moving "outside" and any self-
exposure because of a misunderstood notion about something
"indestructible"—as from any artificial "aggiornamento", any
mindless flirtation with a "difficulty of faith", which one has not
personally experienced but only constructed, or with the *Zeitgeist*.
It is the freely experienced and courageously testifying reliability
and firmness of the believer that shows true solidarity with the
real questions of the unbeliever (even if these take the form
of a bitter polemic). It is even a sign of that honesty, if in the
face of this measurable task the impotence and poverty of any
such attempt by pastoral theology is admitted today in theory
and practice.

Having made these few basic points, let us outline a few ideas
concerning preaching to the unbeliever today.[6]

---

[6] These difficulties might also clearly show how big a subject a truly
pastoral theological investigation is and that this is not to be confused
with a few instructions on pastoral tactics. In the long run, the exertion
of theological thought, which is not to be confused with simply "knocking
a few ideas around", is more profitable for its practical application.

II

BASIC POINTS FOR PREACHING THE WORD
IN A MANNER APPROPRIATE TO THE SITUATION

Suggestions for the proper preaching of the Word should not be taken as referring only to the Sunday sermon. The true insight that all theology is pastoral also operates here, so that the following ideas are concerned with theoretical work on faith and on the lack of faith.

The Proper Understanding of How Life Today in Faith Has Become More Difficult

One cannot preach to the unbeliever in the right way without considering soberly the general intellectual situation of the moment and the corresponding place of the Church in it.[7] It is no longer merely a matter of direct, open observation to discover what the situation today really is and at what points religion and faith could make an impact. The situation is so complicated that the responsible theological interpretation and proclamation of the Gospel today needs a reflective analysis of it. Backward-looking lamentation at the disintegration of a "system of values" that had previously been generally accepted, the rise of a pluralist society indifferent to religion, the growth of the technical mentality of man today which is not receptive to religion, the increase of the "hubris" which is perhaps associated with it, the slow disappearance of any sense of the presence of God in the visible works of creation—all these disappointments, when seen only negatively, cause one to miss the historical moment with its own challenge to a proclamation of faith that is appropriate to it. The world itself is seen in terms of rational understanding, no longer so much as protective "nature" that dwells above men as the presence of God. If man sees everywhere the work and the power of his own hands, only his own reflection in the mirror of the world, then he might sometimes doubt whether all knowledge

[7] Cf. *Handbuch der Pastoraltheologie*, Vol. II/1, pp. 178-276, Vol. II/2, p. 19-45, etc.

and talk of the divine may not ultimately come from human thinking and longing. This makes the "true" God seem further off; at any rate, he loses his anthropomorphic elements and disappears into an ever greater incomprehensibility. Otherwise he would no longer be God.

Let us analyze one particular feature in more detail. The "skepticism" of modern man, for example, should not be characterized in a merely negative way as the unwillingness to commit himself at any deep level. In a world that has become so varied with the thousands of things it offers, great strength of criticism and of distance is necessary—amid the subtly directed infiltrations and ideological manipulations, from the mass media to the most skillful advertising—in order to keep the way open to a truly personal decision (at least in the essential things). Only a "skepticism" that shuts its eyes before many things and preserves for itself in this retreat a little "freedom" can relieve the pressure of the present-day innumerable (nebulous), intellectual offers.

If man today has the same fundamental attitude toward the Church's proclamation, which now exists in an externally leveling situation of intellectual competition without the special privileges of an earlier time, this reserve that is apparently without interest in religious matters should not be automatically regarded as totally deaf and closed to them.

Concern for Theological and Religious Language

In a world that has in this way become Godless,[8] so many new difficulties of understanding arise, so many obvious basic convictions become questionable, that the whole of the Christian message must be thought through anew so that it may in fact appear credible and comprehensible. Man today finds that a very great amount of what the preacher says is "strange", intellectually impenetrable; it is the flotsam and jetsam of past ages. He even objects to such terms as "heaven" and "sin"; he smiles

[8] For the problem of secularization cf. *ibid.*, Vol. II/1. p. 222ff., 242ff.; Vol. II/2, p. 35ff., 40ff., 42ff., 203-67.

at the "virgin birth" and the "ascension"; he is bewildered by such ideas as "indulgences" and the "veneration of saints". Altogether man has the impression that he simply *cannot* believe seriously in such things. The formal answers of previous apologetics are not adequate here. The reason for this failure to understand is not a subjective one of spiritual pride; it is not the foolishness of a man who will not accept this truth of God; but is the objective mysterious character of the truth of faith to which one generally refers "positivistically" when one cannot go any further. On theological grounds, the statements of Vatican Council II concerning atheism make these condemnations and evasions impossible.[9]

Nor is this theological work done on the side "pastorally" by a corresponding didactic method or tactics, but it is concerned with the very foundations of every theological endeavor. The basic hermeneutic structure of theology learns to ask for the meaning of the key words and basic ideas of our kerygma: "God", "grace", "covenant", "succession", "incarnation", etc. These words have been generally overworked, they have become everyday language with many dimensions, ideologically misused and often with their basic significance obscured.[10] Loud propaganda, infringing the laws of discretion precisely in a religious aspect can only do damage here. A banner hung over the street in the middle of all the other advertising signs saying "Don't forget God" only increases the frivolous use of such basically holy words. If one is only slightly aware of the philosophical difficulties of talking about God at all—of the fact that here one is not talking about things within our world that can be given a name, but that this is a reality which makes one fall silent and

---

[9] For the interpretation of the conciliar statements, cf. K. Rahner, "What Does Vatican Council II Teach about Atheism?" in this volume.

[10] This is why the simple repetition of important scriptural words and statements is not sufficient. One frequently hears it said that in the dialogue with atheists a simple return to the words of scripture—far from alienating "metaphysics" and "speculation"—would work wonders. One may doubt the "pastoral" value of this method, even if one is prepared to accept the grain of truth in it and is convinced that scripture is not to be valued any less highly.

yet, in a unique way, is dependent on the Word as the only medium of its presence—then one would have a salutary shock at the careless and frivolous way in which we almost totally ignore this basic insight in our proclamation and theology. In order to realize the difficulty of such language, one does not have to be a skeptical modern philosopher who has passed through Kant and Nietzsche, but it is enough to know the classical *theologia negativa* and the careful doctrine of theological statements held by the mystics (e.g., Master Eckhardt).

Training in the Experience of Faith

However, careful speech is not enough, since the inexpressible, and what has been withdrawn into the area of the intangible, must still be spoken. Today faith still requires a free confession (*parrhesia,* in the sense of St. Paul). If this has become more difficult, then we must simply start at a deeper level. The situation of the experience of the distance of God and of a Godless world itself makes it necessary to have a constant training in the actual religious experience, an introduction to the area of the holy *qua* holy, so that the latter appears automatically within every religious statement and thus attunes the man to recollection and reverence. Contemporary man will be a believer also within the area of his theoretical conviction and his public confession only if he has had a true personal experience of Christianity and is ever anew initiated into it and led further by the Church's proclamation. The world of faith will become less and less merely "doctrine" that is given to men in theological scholarliness and pastoral routine and supported formally by the Church's authority. In a pluralistic society, a system of doctrinal statements and dogmas is no longer supported by a homogeneous public opinion and applied through the common ethos of society. Thus, abstract truths of faith appear easily as subtly elaborated, but concretely unrealizable "realities", which seem more like a pallid ideology that continues to exist for some psychological and sociological reasons but has not had for a long time any power of its own to be transformed into existence. By this "mystagogy into religious experience", as Karl Rahner calls it, we do not mean the hammering in of catechetical knowledge or lecturing to people on ascetic rules of conduct. Spiritual literature and catechesis change only too often into dogmatic speculation and an external conveying of knowledge. The more that direct and traditional popular religiosity disappears, the clearer appears the basic difficulty of making the act of faith, since it now has nothing external to hold on to, so that the requirements of a "higher" spiritual life in earlier times become the minimum condition for a life of faith in a Godless world today.

But faith that is rooted so deeply in the ground of existence must also mean a return to the simple origins of faith. We often find how terribly men torment themselves with the difficulties of peripheral marginal questions and absolute inessentials (e.g., from Mariology, apparitions, etc.). Perhaps they have never had the true religious experience in order to say "Father" and "Thou" to God, or, perhaps, have never in their lives experienced divine grace and divine communication. Many of our marginal questions are solved by themselves or become inessential, if we ourselves grow into the ever greater mystery of God. The honest unbeliever will not then find it quite so easy to criticize our faith when what he sees is not so much the secondary shallows of our beliefs but rather the simple, cautious and sober "yes" to God himself. Here also it is true that everything else is added.

This idea could be pursued further. The initiation into this religious experience would have to be distinguished more clearly from everything that is merely "doctrinaire": that faith is free, obscure, and given totally in grace, would have to be worked out in detail, as well as all the statements of traditional theology that nevertheless play a remarkably small role in our concrete Christian thinking and action. We should have to consider the possibilities of the religious instruction of adults, the limits of an ethics of law, the introduction into the deeper significance of a more frequent reception of the sacraments, the caution necessary in appealing directly to the "will" of God, etc.

The Rooting of Faith in Everyday Life

A preliminary outline of principles requires taking a further step. If the rooting of a life of faith in religious experience is a basic requirement of Christian living in the world today, this experience itself should not be found in a false and pseudo-mystical cult of inwardness, which finally is concerned only with pious emotions and subjective religious feelings (which cannot be investigated). Piety must be made public and secular. The affinity of our human, secular and non-holy self-experience to life in faith, hope and love must be made fruitful. The appearance that faith is only an ideological superstructure can be removed only by the total rooting of the life in grace within ordinary everyday life. But here we must avoid a misunderstanding. This placing of faith within the ordinariness of daily life does not mean in any way a legalistic reshaping of the secular events of the day in their ordinary course by the mere "applications" of external maxims and principles of Christian morality or dogmatism. Faith is not something from a high realm that comes down over everything like a mystical veil. The place for God's grace is in the midst of the insignificance and meanness of everyday activity. Revelation is also the interpretation of our own sense of existence; God can really reach us. It would lead us too far if we wanted to give a theological justification of this experience of grace in everyday life. Let us say merely that faith does not lie simply beyond the actual, conscious and free acts of living, even if it cannot always be grasped thematically in reflection.[11] Wherever a man out of the innermost fidelity to his task and in the knowledge of the necessity of what he does for his fellowmen, devotes himself quietly and unselfishly in his work; where, after being immeasurably disappointed by those who are near to one, a new stretch of life together is traversed, against all hope; where, against all the laws of the experience of this world an important work is begun and performed that remains nameless and unrewarded; where a misunderstood and lonely conscience must go its painful way with-

[11] Cf. the further detail in K. Rahner, *Schriften zur Theologie* III (Einsiedeln, 1964), pp. 105-9.

out recognition—in these situations in life and in many thousands of other similar ones there is an experience of the eternity and of the grace of God, even if there are no high-sounding words spoken. On the contrary, in this sober school great programs are torn up; all self-advertising fuss and gesticulating soon prove hollow and empty. Perhaps we do not even need to turn around to see this eternal life in our own lives and to "enjoy" it with inner satisfaction. You can find grace only if you forget yourself. This "mysticism" of everyday life is as hard, sober and factual as that.[12] It is the real school of faith and the test for the Christian in relation to the unbeliever.

Here faith can become "secular" in a fresh way: by letting the experiences of humanity be drawn into the ways of the greater grace of God.

Introduction to the Proper Way of Praying

There is still something to be said concerning the kerygma and the introduction to prayer. Here also one will not start from fixed formulas of prayer that have nothing to do immediately with real life, or else whose real, secret connection with it has not yet been mentally grasped. It is not easy to know what prayer is, not easy to wait until man has gotten rid of the secret suspicion that it is nothing but a good psychological means of comfort by talking persuasively to oneself; one great "projection" which is content to imagine that what is fervently longed for, but not yet attainable, is still hidden afar off; just the sign of a pre-rational and childlike way of dealing with life, which only seeks to put a veil over the naked brutality of the facts. Here also over-luxuriant piety must be reduced to simplicity: the cry of man from the depths of his distress, perhaps a cry of despair; a "yes", wrung painfully from him, in the face of a difficult decision; the confession of faith long fought over in his conscience and the acknowledgment of grave guilt; smiling contentment and quiet satisfaction at a good deed that has been successful; gay rejoicing at

[12] Cf. the practical essay by K. Rahner, *Alltägliche Dinge* (Einsiedeln, 1966); also the essay by T. Steeman in this volume.

an unexpected happiness. If this kind of thing happens in stammering words or in the inaudible language of the heart, then prayer is there already.

We Christians articulate too little the reality of the experience of grace in and through prayer. Who takes seriously the fact that not only the sacrament of penance but even the reverent praying of the *Confiteor* can be the event of the forgiveness of sin; that God, if we will only try to look up to him, says more in our wordless silence than we can understand? It is from this insight into God's saving deed toward us through our mental prayer that more explicit prayer comes: the call from the particular situation; the knowledge that one has been summoned by God to continue courageously with one's task along the path of life; the memory of the powerful working of God in history in one's own and in other people's lives: the moving and thankful account of God's saving deed.

Considerateness and Solidarity

Thus, in the proclamation of his faith in word and deed, the Christian does not need to maneuver himself into a special, sacrificial theology if he desires to encounter today's unbeliever. Only our concrete historical situation must pass into the contemporary form of faith: we must face the demands of the day ever anew, soberly and humbly. "This faith must be such that even the so-called unbeliever cannot deny that here a man believes who is like himself; a man of today, who does not speak the word 'God' easily or frivolously, who does not assume that he has grasped this mystery; a modest, cool, skeptical man, a man of today like himself, who despite this—no, not despite this but just because of this—believes. Our faith must appear before the so-called unbelievers as fraternal love." [13]

This solidarity does not exclude a tough dispute, if it is a matter of showing the other that his thinking does not ask what the world and Christianity are in reality, and if only preconceived

[13] K. Rahner, *Im Heute glauben,* 2nd ed. (Einsiedeln, 1966), p. 21.

opinions, maxims, and secondary objectivations have crowded out the thing itself. But all necessary controversy will have to be conducted without the tone of inner superiority, if the unbeliever is to be addressed not only externally, but is to be able to hear again and be receptive. If at the end he has an ambiguous feeling that the Christian does not apparently hold any narrow "dogmas", then the proclamation has been a good one, without the proclaimer having to be reproached with abbreviating the Christian Gospel.

<h2 style="text-align:center">III</h2>

<h3 style="text-align:center">NORMS OF THE CHRISTIAN BEHAVIOR TOWARD THE UNBELIEVER IN SOCIAL LIFE</h3>

The proclamation to the unbeliever, in particular, is very often not made only in a direct address that has a definite religious character, but, above all, in the dimension of the social and political presence of the Church as a whole. But if "preaching" (in the sense of any public proclamation) becomes less important as the medium of encounter (although all the demands we have mentioned are still valid in full measure and with full weight), then the concrete form of this ecclesial "presence" in the social sphere is to be taken account of all the more. Hence, let us, in conclusion, formulate a few principles for the proper effectiveness of this indirect proclamation.[14]

The Privilege of Faith in Social and Political Forms

In present-day society the Church is no longer an entity that can influence the social sector as a whole or even in large measure. If this situation is undoubtedly a danger for the faith of the many—which cannot itself be lightly passed over, even for real

---

[14] In more detail in *Handbuch der Pastoraltheologie*, Vol. II/1, pp. 259-67.

pastoral reasons—then on the whole we see something positive in terms of salvation history, even if this does not follow from the situation with mechanical necessity: the radicalization of the question of faith is the opportunity for faith to find in personal decision its true nature and its original genuineness. That does not mean giving up the missionary task, or a call for a Church of the spiritual elite and enthusiasts, or giving up its institutional side.[15] But in practice this means that the Christian—in whatever situation he is—must openly and courageously fight for possibly small but, for that reason, living community of believers, if it is a matter of the relation of the Church to social positions. Holding fast to traditional positions of power only leads to resentments, to the intensification of anti-clerical emotions and other tensions.

This situation also involves giving up many social functions that the Church formerly performed. From a purely external point of view, the Church can no longer look after the many areas of secular life that were formerly her province (e.g., schools, science, social institutions, etc.). Traditional preserves should not be overestimated, because in the complex structure of contemporary society there are many possibilities of exchange and mutual influence between areas that once had little to do with one another (cf., for example, the educational influence of the mass media on youth, who no longer acquire their knowledge only from parents who are believers and from a "denominational" school).

Inter-Church Freedom and Brotherliness

A homogeneously Christian society created special privileges for certain classes. In today's society the social prestige of the Church and of its office holders is necessarily smaller. If we have grasped that this historical development is irreversible, then no serious Christian who cares about the spread of the faith will

[15] Cf. *ibid.*, Vol. II/2, p. 153ff., 161ff.

want to defend these privileges against the whole of society. With this exterior sociological change, interior rethinking also becomes necessary: the Church hierarchy (from deacon to pope) will inevitably appear in a far greater degree as service in humility and self-limitation. When earthly honor and social positions vanish, and the acknowledged power of tradition is reduced, then the relationship to the group of personally and freely believing men will be a fraternal community. Authority will not be questioned, but will become concerned to engender a spirit of absolute objectivity, of trust and understanding in making decisions.[16] Only in such an atmosphere will the unbeliever gain the impression that a real community of believers exists, not the authoritarian administration and "taking care" of immature people. Since the Church is more than ever dependent on the layman in order to be able to guarantee the presence of the Church in the life of the world, it becomes even more urgent to take account of these claims. If it brings no advantages of any kind to be a member of a Church, then neither unnecessary difficulties should be created nor any superfluous resistance should build up. The strength of the believing and loving members of the Church itself is socially the only truly fruitful power of the Church.

The Opportunity for Difficult Dialogue

This view does not imply pessimism or tendencies to shut oneself off in the ghetto of an esoteric group. The Church is forbidden by its missionary task to do that. It will seek contact with every social group; it will, by cooperating in many different areas of life be in a direct exchange of experience with people who think differently. Such a dialogue today[17] looks different from the former. Perhaps it will never come to an end, even though it is not undertaken out of a simple desire to speak, but in order to

[16] Cf. the numerous writings of Y. Congar on the necessary spirit of service in the Church. Cf. also K. Rahner, *Vom Sinn kirchlicher Hierarchie* (Freiburg, 1966).

[17] Cf. K. Rahner, *"Über den dialog in der pluralistischen Gesellschaft,"* in *Schriften zur Theologie* VI (Einsieldeln, 1965), pp. 46-58.

tell the other person the uniquely healing truth. Yet the present situation is that no one knows everything any more; therefore, he can always learn from the other. If we say that our fellow men also stand beneath the general saving will of God, and so do not speak, of themselves, only the direct opposite of the truth, then the Church that learns by means of this dialogue can be led deeper into her own truth. Thus, old truth can be liberated from prejudices associated with it, and new perspectives will arise, etc.

The Test of the Deed

But all this is not enough. There is not only the evidence of theory, but even more of the concrete act. Everything we have said so far could be merely tactics, a social rule of the game in the name of self-preservation. The fact of truly personal love of one's neighbor that involves one's whole being is the basic conviction of the truth of faith and constant de-ideologization of one's own theories, objectivizations and wrong mental attitudes. "Love of one's neighbor" should not be prettified into an out-of-date gesture of condescending to give alms. Not even the simple and inconspicuous act for one's unknown neighbor is sufficient, however important this particular witness is. It is a question of moving out, of liberating oneself from inhuman situations of every kind, so that this "love of one's neighbor" also has a unique "political" dimension. It is a question of real "action". The quietistic attitude of the Christian to the problem of society in past times is not the least of the reasons for the growth of unbelief. The world expects Christians to open their mouths when violence and injustice occur. This is the right place for "anathematization". The world will no longer tolerate any turning away to the eternal, as long as we are failing our fellow men. The protest of the unbeliever is largely directed, not against faith, but against its misuse in politics. A false trust in history deceived the hopes of men, made deprivation and oppression fatalistically attractive and valuable as acceptance of the will of God. Christians have often suppressed the revolutionary elements of their faith;

they have not used their royal freedom and their hope which opens up the future.[18]

This revolution needs a special kind of serenity. The Christian knows the hiddenness of the eschatological fulfillment. Hence, he will not only radically change himself, his Church, the truly secondary scandals (faith itself remains the irremovable *scandalum crucis*) of the Church's history into good, but also unmask and de-ideologize the secular utopias. He will certainly do all he can to further the excellent humanitarian programs and human happiness generally, but in his knowledge of the power of sin and death he will also declare that the resistance of reality is harder, that man always stands in his own way, that he always rushes to use terror in order to establish paradise by force. The inner equilibrium of faith, hope and love helps the Christian to make a protest against all reconciliation by force or blackmail simply by means of human manipulation and planning.[19]

Thus, there is much solidarity with today's unbeliever. Pseudo-intellectual fraternization, romantic attachment to one's foreign brothers and the busy special pastoral work of "specialists in unbelief" all equally miss the point. For us there remains in this difficult dialogue only the possibility of making our own house a little more respectable and inviting. This is all we need to do at the moment, and this offers the best preparation for dialogue. What does the unbeliever expect of us? Something simple that destroys any modish curiosity for anything like an artificially bolstered up "dialogue with unbelievers", and reveals many wrong investments in contemporary endeavors to which it aims: "The world today requires of Christians that they remain Christians." Albert Camus, one of the most attractive figures of contemporary "unbelief", hit the nail right on the head.[20] This is our

---

[18] Cf. J. B. Metz, "Gott vor uns", in *Ernst Bloch zu ehren* (Frankfurt, 1965), pp. 227-41; *idem,* "Verantwortung der Hoffnung," in *Stimmen der Zeit* 91 (1966).

[19] Cf. K. Rahner, "Experiment Mensch. Theologisches zur Selbstmanipulation des Menschen," in *Die Frage nach dem Menschen. Festschrift für M. Müller*, ed. by H. Rombach (Freiburg, 1966), pp. 45-69.

[20] Cf. A. Camus, *Fragen der Zeit* (Reinbek bei Hamburg), 1960, p. 74.

old and ever new task, both simple and almost impossible. This is the beginning of our responsibility for the proclamation of the faith to unbelievers[21] with our very first greeting, with the earnestness of our prayer, with the sermon tomorrow, and with all that we leave out in between—out of the weakness of our faith, which shows our own persistent unbelief.

[21] For concrete pastoral and catechetical work we recommend two recent books: E. Feifel, *Die Glaubensunterweisung und der abwesende Gott* (Freiburg, 1965); K. Tilmann, *Das Glaubensgespräch mit Andern* (Würzburg, 1966).

Jacques Loew/ *Toulouse, France*

Personal, Pastoral Contact with the Non-Believer

66"The fool says in his heart: 'There is no God.' " [1] Undoubtedly, there are always unbelievers of this sort, but they are rarely those whom the priest meets in his ordinary ministry.

With engaged couples who come to ask their parish priest, not for the *sacrament,* but for a marriage *service,* and admit, if they are at ease with the priest, that faith and God have no importance or interest for them; in the interview before baptism, when the husband explains that this concerns the wife, it's no business of his; in daily conversations when religion is dismissed as "out of date"—it is always, though in many different ways, fundamentally the same: they are not interested in God.

As Madeleine Debrel wrote, summing up in a trenchant account thirty years of life shared with atheism, it is the man-with-matter relation that in practice holds and captures the attention of our contemporaries.

"This relation is established in a total silence with regard to God. By a strange substitution, creation fills the place of the creator. This silence does not alarm us as it should. A grave danger is silently menacing the Church: the danger of a time, a world, in which God will no longer be denied, no longer driven away, but shut out, unthinkable." [2]

[1] Psalm 14.
[2] M. Debrel, *Nous autres, gens des rues,* p. 275, footnote 1.

Generally the non-believer approaches the priest as he approaches an employee or an official over some formality to be arranged: in such a case it matters little what the person is like, provided one obtains what one wants with the least possible complication. Sometimes it is the priest who takes the initiative with a visit about a child and catechetical instruction, or just a pastoral visit. If the priest's arrival occurs when the man has just returned from a tiring day, or in competition with an exciting television program, the visitor seems an intruder and dialogue is scarcely possible. Or again, if the meeting is called on public business, about some joint social action, or a movement in which believers and non-believers take part, all their effort will be absorbed by the movement and the common aim.

Much easier and more straightforward are the contacts between the priest doing a manual job with his co-workers, or the relations of neighbors in a district. But these cases are still exceptional and outside the usual pastoral contacts.

We must face it: the ideal meeting between the priest and the non-believer, one that is relaxed and unequivocal, rarely takes place, and this is only to be expected, for to one of the parties God is all, to the other he is unimportant and even boring.

I

How Can We Transform Contacts or "Transactions" into Real Human Relations?

Anything which directly or indirectly smacks of the artificial, of the "dodge" on the priest's part, rings false and is condemned, as much by God as by the unbeliever. Seeking or devising points of contact is sterile, as soon as it assumes the style of a contrived method of attraction, and that is only fair. The priest who, consciously or unconsciously, tries to show that he is not just "half a man" (and which of us has not at some time been so tempted?) may dazzle, perhaps, but where will that lead? To himself, not to our Lord.

And yet it is precisely a man whom the non-believer must find at first, for while, in the end, it is the Word of God he must discover, it is through a man that this discovery must take place, a man who believes. This is to state the importance of the man, the human, in the dialogue that is started. For this, the non-believer must find in the priest a man naturally open to all that is beautiful, great and noble in science, in art, in discoveries, in technology; a man sharing in the feelings of justice and legitimate indignation in the presence of wrong, of compassion in the presence of suffering; a man, in short, of hope and (in the best sense of the word) of heart.

This does not happen in a vacuum. With engaged couples it will be from their love; with a young father, from his responsibilities; with a keen trade unionist, from solidarity; or, with a mind interested in such things, from the origins of man or the world. All these are so many points from which the dialogue can start.

The priest can then say what his faith strengthens, or extends, or cures, in these great realities. But a snare remains: the danger of confining God and reducing him to our problems and our human measures. God, of course, is "present in the event"— justice, love, devotion, the universe—but he is God only on condition that he bursts asunder our current forms and categories. He is always "he who by the power at work within us is able to do far more abundantly than all we ask or think . . ." [3] Here there is a margin of grandeur and mystery, in which the priest must be so steeped that it will appear even through his attention to the cares and aspirations of the other. It is a matter of common sensibility, profound interest that does not lie because it was there before they met. It is, above all, a capacity to listen with love (*benevolentia!*) to what the other tells you, on the pattern of Mary, who "kept all these things, pondering them in her heart".

A priest who had been working for only a few weeks in a factory in Brazil, had not had an opportunity to tell his com-

[3] Eph. 3, 20.

panions who he was; they only knew him as "Paolo the turner", and learned his identity only the day after he was killed in a fatal accident. After the first moment of astonishment they said: "Ah, now we know why he was so attentive and listened so well." They spontaneously connected that quality, which had struck them in their friend, with his priesthood.

In all this, the priest acts as the man who is neighbor to his brother. That is the real substructure that must exist first, and its virtue can transform a casual, sometimes compulsory contact, into an encounter that will at least be remembered as a meeting of man with man. A family doctor can be a neighbor to his patient; an overworked doctor in charge of a dispensary or of an understaffed hospital service is in danger of becoming, against his will, simply a curer. In the same way, the priest must be sufficiently at people's disposal to "rejoice together, to weep together". This takes time, and does not find a place in collective programs.

II

THE PRIEST'S "JOB"

This communion with the non-believer, in persons and things, has nothing idyllic about it. Whether it is over a sacrament to be received, a choice to be made or a policy involving joint action, at some point, differences are bound to occur.

Here the priest's "job" brings him up against the requirements or aspirations of the non-believer. It is the painful moment for the priest when, like St. Paul at Athens, he is told: "We will hear you another time," or when he himself has to refuse something to one who cannot understand the refusal.

It seems to me that this difficulty, which belongs to the very "job" of the priest, can produce at least something positive: the perception of the real dimension of the priesthood. An artisan, however humble his job, is thought to be skilled if he has that knowledge, that perfect mastery of his craft which enables him to be excited about it and eager to explain it to others. It is the same for the priest. A man may not be able to share his faith, but he can find him to be an impassioned servant of the sacred, an enthusiast in the search for God, who longs to communicate his permanent discoveries, the religious man, the mediator, the *pontifex,* the one who builds bridges, from earth to heaven, from heaven to earth.

When a man comes expecting to find someone to carry out a formality, he should find in the priest quite another dimension, that of a man who is at home in the bible, like the petroleum expert in his operations of distilling and refining oils, who knows what is happening and what it means: one who relies on the Word even more than the engineer on his calculations. He does not excel in erudition, but in his attention to the Master.

He is not a man who presents the Church as a herbarium or a textbook of anatomy; he is a living man who receives his life from that many-functioned body and shows that he himself is a member of that Church. And if one points out the stains or the diseases of that body, one can see that he is a man who has reflected on the treacheries of man and the faithfulness of God. What matters is not primarily the subject of discussion, but the man whom the non-believer can see to be living, sure of his faith and modest at the same time; neither a propagandist for a group nor a preacher of an ideology, but one who, to the best of his power, transmits the deposit (of faith): "I received from the Lord what I also delivered to you . . ." [4] And with all this, "unfailing in patience and in teaching", as St. Paul recommended to Timothy.

Here the pastoral encounter depends less on any doctrine than on that "still more excellent way", the charity the priest is able to instill into his contacts.

I have quoted Madeleine Debrel for a definition of nonbelief; now I quote her to tell what the meeting with goodness can accomplish.

[4] 1 Cor. 11, 23.

"Nothing in the world can give us the goodness of Christ save Christ himself. Nothing in the world can give us access to our neighbor's heart, but the fact that we have given Christ access to our own.

"The goodness of the heart of Christ, given by him, is to the non-believer's heart a presentment of God himself. To that heart it has the unknown taste of God, and it makes him sensitive to his approach. To the non-believer it is unfamiliar, linked to that absolute unfamiliarity which God is to him. It rouses and challenges the dormant powers of his heart, those powers unknown to him, whose living reality he perceives in himself. It sympathizes with that element in the non-believer's heart, which is both the most solitary and the most apt to be turned inwardly, secretly, toward God as a possibility." [5]

III

THE MAN OF CERTAINTIES

There is another point to be emphasized, a trap to be avoided. The non-believer may have vague ideas about the Church's faith, but he is bound to have heard talk about many questions raised by Christians today, before, during and after the Council. Apart from distortions sometimes introduced by political passion, there are so many "problems" that come to mind whenever religion is mentioned: pope, bishops, curia, priests and celibacy, ecumenism, dialogue with Marxism, the atom bomb, divorce and the pill, the social attitudes of the episcopate, Schema XIII—everything, in short, which must be included in the general *aggiornamento*.

Now, as regards the non-believer, all these problems presented as problems drown the essence of the saving message. The words of Psalm 12 (in a possible translation of the old Vulgate): "Save us, O Lord . . . for certainties are diminished among the children of men", give us the key to the missionary attitude in view

[5] M. Debrel, *op. cit.*, p. 294.

of the "absence of God" from the world. If there is any possibility today of being the instrument of God toward those who are indifferent, it lies in the extent to which certainties flow naturally from the priest, certainties founded on the unshakeable rock of God and the faith.

What have we to offer to one who is indifferent, if we embark with him (even at his invitation) on subjects debated among Christians? At best, if he really has goodwill, he will realize that the Church is modernizing herself ("for fear of losing her members?"); but it is not from this point that the primordial truths of the faith will arise and burst upon him, the faith which is *the* truth that makes one (want) *to be* a Christian.

The non-believer, the indifferent, will not be touched at the deepest level of his soul by even the best *aggiornamento; metanoia,* the change of heart, will not come from that. While the Council is reconciling the world to the Church, and because it is doing so, we must stake our all more boldly on the essential truths, and be heralds of the certainties that have been given us, not the propounders of problems that are always the normal field of the experts.

An unexpected confirmation of this conviction was given me by Karl Barth in an interview on the occasion of his eightieth birthday, when he declared:

"To a pastor beginning his ministry today I should say: To be a witness, one must know that to which one is witnessing. Pastors often think they have the Gospel in their pockets. Their thoughts revolve around the question, *how* to present the Gospel. To my mind the great question is not the 'how'—whether to be more or less modern, more or less liturgical, more or less philosophical—but the 'what'. They must present something strange, surprising, and the Gospel is a strange thing. But to discover it, that takes work. . . .

"Once the Gospel was presented in the form of law, now it is as a message of freedom. . . .

"But perhaps it is difficult today to understand that this

freedom is a freedom in obedience. Today men float. But to float is not to be free; it is to be the prisoner of all the waves that flow. Only the communion of saints can uphold us today, not the political or social communion.

"Today men are going to the moon, around the moon, but it doesn't make much difference to our human condition. Those who bear responsibility in the Church must not lose themselves in time or space; they must concentrate on the reality of the living God; that is what men need." [6]

In the last resort, the contact will be illuminated by a supernatural realism, restoring the transcendence to God, to his mystery of salvation, to our Lord, to man. What will cause the indifferent to think is not the solution we offer to his problems, but his finding the priest to be a man like the one in the parable who, having discovered the treasure, went away full of joy. That is how the priest can be infectious in his faith, when the treasure he has discovered enraptures him to such a point that this rapture becomes the sign that the treasure itself is incomparable.

The effect on persons troubled by problems of meeting a man who lives by certainties has been very well analyzed by a husband and wife, converts, and godchildren of Léon Bloy:

". . . to be able to be witnesses of the life of a man in whom we could see—in his everyday life, like breath in the body—the incarnation of all that obscure reality of the faith. No doubt we were reflecting on it, asking ourselves questions and reading books about the faith and the Catholic religion. But only a man of flesh and blood, placed at the heart of the hard, daily reality, and living by God as a plant lives by the light, could convince us what a power of life was contained in Catholicism and give form to the desire which was urging us on.

[6] Interview given on May 10, 1966 by Karl Barth, on his eightieth birthday, *Bulletin du Conseil Oecuménique des Eglises*, (Bulletin of the World Council of Churches) = SOEPI, May 12, n. 15, pp. 3 and 4.

". . . Once we had entered the Bloys' home, all that we knew in this world, all the richness of life, material existence, men, things, all these became unreal, seemed perfectly artificial. Yet, at the same time everything acquired its genuine, true, perfectly simple reality." [7]

The two conditions outlined by Pierre and Christine van der Meer admirably sum up what the personal, pastoral contact with non-belief can be, as I have tried to express it in these pages.

"A man of flesh and blood, placed at the heart of the hard, daily reality"; there you have all the attention to things, the sensibility, the capacity to be enthralled by all that makes up the life of men.

"Living by God as a plant lives by the light"; that is what Jacques Maritain also comments on, speaking of his godfather, Léon Bloy: "What he revealed to them can never be told; the tenderness of Christian brotherhood, and that kind of trembling mercy and fear which possessed his soul, stamped with the love of God, in the presence of another soul." [8]

I know that we shall not often meet people like Pierre and Christine van der Meer, or Jacques and Raïssa Maritain, and no one of us is Léon Bloy! But what other path can we hope to follow, if we are to present the fact of God, however distantly, to the non-believer?

[7] P. van der Meer De Walcheren, *Rencontres* (Paris: Desclée de Brouwer, 1961), pp. 152-3.

[8] J. Maritain. (Introduction). *Pages de Léon Bloy* (Mercure de France ed., 1951).

Paul Matussek / *Munich, West Germany*

The Function of the Sermon with Regard to Repressed Unbelief in the Believer

I

A DEFINITION OF THE TERMS EMPLOYED

In connection with the subject for discussion proposed by the editor, we must first of all clarify what is understood by "repression" in the believer. The word repression, originally coined by Freud to characterize certain clearly defined psychic mechanisms, is nowadays used in a looser sense, and this has caused many misunderstandings.

Repression and Suppression

The process that is quite commonly regarded as repression, even by modern moral and pastoral theologians, is more accurately described by the psychoanalyst as suppression. This process consists of a more or less conscious rejection of some knowledge or other from the level of consciousness. The person concerned, therefore, retains, however dimly, some awareness of what he has rejected. Illustrative of this process in the realm of moral and pastoral theology are, for example, the "sinful" fantasies (*delectationes morosae*) which are known to us all and which we should try with all our strength to banish from our minds.

This kind of suppression must be distinguished from actual repression, which takes place on an unconscious level, that is, the person concerned knows nothing about his repression, neither its process nor its contents. Certain mechanisms perform this function "automatically", as a defense for the ego. In such cases psychoanalysis distinguishes between stronger and weaker repressions. The strength of a repression is usually measured according to the degree of resistance encountered by the analyst in attempting to bring to the surface of the conscious mind what has been repressed. But psychoanalysis is not the only means by which this may be achieved. Conditions that weaken the defense-mechanisms (e.g. illness, exhaustion, sleep) or increase the pressure from within of what is being repressed (e.g. certain "occasions of temptation") can also have the same effect. Not only for the doctor and the psychotherapist, therefore, but also for the moral and pastoral theologian, repression is in one respect more interesting than suppression. For, whereas suppression has to do with a more or less conscious effort of the mind and seldom has any serious pathological consequences, repression can very easily reduce the person concerned to a pathological condition (though it does not necessarily do so).

Repressed Unbelief

For the subject of our discussion we shall take the problem of repressed unbelief. By "unbelief" we do not mean the reverse of that function of believing inherent in the nature of man—the loss of any such faculty for belief is only conceivable in the most serious pathological cases—but rather what we might call "material" unbelief, that is, the unbelief that rejects specific ideas, such as the existence of God or the doctrines of the Church. It must be stressed that such repressed unbelief can both involve a sense of moral guilt and also arise from a subjective attitude to the problem of making a free decision about matters of faith. The distinction between these two factors in repressed unbelief is of course very important, but since they both come within the sphere of influence of the preacher they may be considered together here.

The way in which unbelief is repressed, and what the consequences of such a repression are, cannot easily be presented under a schematic heading. Something must be known of the life of the person concerned and the situation that led to the repression in order to understand so complex a phenomenon as that of belief or unbelief.

Instead of a systematic investigation, therefore, let us take a particular case that will illustrate one form of repressed unbelief. A thirty-two-year-old priest had experienced a growing compulsion over several years to blaspheme and give expression to obscene thoughts while praying, and even during Mass. When all attempts in the way of spiritual exercises to overcome the temptation proved ineffective, he was persuaded to undergo psychotherapeutic treatment. After a year and a half of treatment the symptoms disappeared. What is interesting for us in this case is the unbelief deeply anchored in the personality of the priest, but which he would not acknowledge. On the contrary, he considered himself a fervent believer whom the devil harassed with insane thoughts. It was some time before he ceased to blame the devil for his symptoms and instead made the sickness of his mind responsible for them. This idea afforded him a certain relief insofar as he did not need to feel personally responsible for them. In the course of the therapy, however, even this discovery came to be modified. The patient was obliged to realize that neither the devil nor any sickness of which he was the innocent victim had forced these blasphemies upon him, but that he himself was responsible for them. He was gradually able to admit to himself that behind his conscious conviction that he was a believer lay a deep unbelief. The more he came to full realization of this unbelief, the freer he inwardly became, so that he was eventually able to make a free decision with regard to his faith and his priestly calling.

In this short account of a particular case it was not intended to show that unbelief was the sole cause of the neurosis. No neurosis is so simple in its origins that it can be explained or understood from only one aspect (such as sexuality, unbelief, aggression, and the like). The compulsive neurosis, as in the case described, could be the exception rather than the rule as the powerful motivating force of a repressed unbelief. Nevertheless, the ability to accept the fact of repressed unbelief plays an important role in the therapeutic process. We have mentioned this case to show that in such instances of repressed unbelief, which have pathological consequences, the preacher is hardly likely to be able to exert any influence. Only therapeutic measures can help here.

Pious Self-Acceptance and Latent Unbelief

The influence of the preacher is more likely to be effective in those cases of repressed unbelief among followers of the faith, which I have described in detail in my discussion with the Catholic moral theologian, Egenter.[1]

The people in question are the considerable number of churchgoers who consider themselves good Catholics. They fulfill the obligations imposed on them by the Church without any great difficulty. If one reproaches them with the fact that their faith does not exert a very profound influence over their lives, because the contradictions between their behavior and the profession of belief are so glaring, they are usually not very surprised. They are often quick to reply that they are not conscious of any serious failings, and they disassociate themselves from any of the grave sins that might be charged to those in their immediate or wider environment. They also readily admit that they are in no way perfect and could never hope to be. Having ascertained this, they are then usually content to ignore or put aside the problem of an inner contradiction—on the one hand, a pious self-acceptance, on the other, a latent unbelief, which is not recognized precisely because all the "rules of the faith" seem to be dutifully adhered to. The psychotherapist only rarely encounters such people in his practice. Repressed unbelief resulting from

[1] R. Egenter and P. Matussek, *Ideologie, Glaube und Gewissen*, 2nd edition (Munich, 1965).

an ideological attitude to faith does not in general lead to symptoms that have any medical relevance. The doctor usually encounters such people only indirectly, for example, in certain
symptoms that manifest themselves in their children.

II

THE DUTY INCUMBENT ON THE PREACHER

If, on the strength of this minimal experience (minimal from
a psychotherapeutic point of view), one were to ask what part
the influence of a preacher could play, one should perhaps
remember first and foremost that the people of whom we are
speaking often feel themselves supported in their deficient attitude to their faith by what they hear from the pulpit. Undoubtedly, there are many opportunities for influence. First, let
us illustrate the problem by reference to the relationship between
the literal observance of the moral code and latent unbelief.

The Appeal from the Pulpit and Latent Unbelief

Because a church-goer never seriously feels that the morality of
his way of life is called into question or in any way threatened
by the pulpit appeal to his conscience, his moral feelings are too
quiescent and repressed to bring his latent unbelief to the surface.
One simply cannot claim that by preaching the moral norms,
the Church reveals the contradiction between these norms and
the moral life of the average believer. Only too often the
preacher fails to arouse the conscience of his listeners, and the
kind of sermon preached is often such, that the contradiction
between the ideal and the reality is felt to be "normal", fundamentally unavoidable and, therefore, not in the least disturbing.
The sermon is usually much too concerned with individual demands, and does not have the effect of a challenge to make a
radical decision in matters of faith. Even less does the average
sermon make clear the fact that moral respectability can become
a means of concealing from the church-goer himself and from

the people in his immediate environment his deep-lying lack of faith.[2]

The Confession of Sinfulness and Unbelief in the Church

In many sermons the Church is presented to the believer simply as an infallible and unchanging institution. The theological distinction of the infallibility with regard to certain well-defined doctrines, is only vaguely understood by many people, if at all. As a result, the believer accepts as infallible and unchanging or, as an authoritative statement on the Christian way of life, all that which is frequently no more than a private opinion or attitude of the preacher or the average church-goer and which is quite often even false from a theological or moral point of view.

The contribution that the preacher unwittingly makes to the repression of unbelief could therefore be evident wherever the sermon encourages a repression of unbelief in the Church instead of attempting to overcome it. The description of the Church as an institution made up entirely of true believers corresponds neither to the facts nor to what sober and critical theologians of our own time have had the courage to say.[3] The Church is indeed aware of her sinfulness and of the divergence of opinion in matters of faith among those official representatives who have

[2] Of course, it cannot be denied that there are misconceptions of a moral nature which from an abstract point of view do not affect the idea of unbelief in a theological sense (see. *Denz.* 837). But our concern here is that in the actual activities of our daily lives the failure to make real moral decisions gives an inner motivating force to latent unbelief in the theological sense. This is especially the case today, because faith and belief in modern society are not supported by a public and general conviction, with the result that a decision or attitude in questions of morality develops much more easily and quickly than in earlier ages into actual unbelief. This unbelief is of course nonetheless powerful for being suppressed or repressed.

[3] Cf. K. Rahner, "Gerecht und Sünder zugleich," "Kirche der Sünder," "Sündige Kirche nach den Dekraten des Zweiten Vatikanischen Konzils," in *Schriften zur Theologie* VI (Einsiedeln, 1965), pp. 212-76, 301-20, 321-47. For the idea of unbelief, cf. J. Metz, "Unbelief as a Theological Problem," in *Concilium Vol. 6: The Church and the World* (Glen Rock, N.J.: Paulist Press, 1966) pp. 59-77; cf. *idem*, "Unglaube II", *Lex. Theol. u. Kirche* X, 2nd edition (Freiburg, 1965), pp. 496-99.

the powers of decision. She is also aware—at least theoretically—that there is sin among her ranks, and with sin, unbelief. From the standpoint of a preacher's audience, however, the theoretical knowledge of sin and of the concomitant unbelief in the Church does not suffice to enable the believer to confront himself with his own unbelief. On the contrary, continuous talk of general sinfulness, which does not necessarily exclude belief, leads rather to a concealment of the relevant problems.

Admitting the Liability of the Preacher to Error

Just as with repressed unbelief in the Church as an official institution, so also repressed unbelief in the preacher must be brought to light, in order to prevent the regular church-goer from receiving the impression that the preacher is not like other men and does not also stand in constant danger of lapsing into unbelief. To be sure, one might ask how a man who is meant to proclaim the faith can preach about it, if he is going to talk also of his own unbelief. Would he not be casting doubt on his own words? The fear inherent in such questions could in fact be considered very convincing evidence of a state of repressed unbelief. The "believer" would then receive the impression that the exemplary kind of belief is not prepared to acknowledge whatever elements of unbelief are contained in it. He would further receive the impression that he must repress his own unbelief if he wishes to count himself, for whatever reasons, among the number of the faithful.

The Danger of Not Recognizing Unbelief

In some sermons, as in these tracts of a devotional and edifying nature with which we are all acquainted, reference is frequently made to unbelievers who shortly before dying find their way back to the Church and thereby become conscious of, and overcome, their repressed unbelief in the face of death. Mention was earlier made of the fact that repression or defense mechanisms are often weakened or removed during illness and times of physical weakness. Such conditions of physical weakness are often, of course, experienced before a person finally dies. It can happen that as a result of such a condition, the unbelief that has been repressed a whole life long will erupt in an elemental way. Whoever has had the opportunity of observing such cases frequently will certainly have grounds to pause and consider what it is that can cause so violent a change at the end of such a "pious", "faithful" and "exemplary" life.

Not until our own day has moral theology gradually become more open to such problems and ceased to be satisfied with simply ascribing them to the inscrutable decrees of God. Today the psychological reasons for such phenomena are examined and, with the aid of depth psychology, repressed unbelief can be discovered and treated. Knowledge of the psychological significance of such manifestations should make the preacher more aware of his own "unbelief"; it should enable him to use this knowledge in his sermons in such a way that those whom he is addressing may realize that even he has to struggle for his faith; for, even the priest does not receive faith as an immutable gift. A vicar-general once told me that the unbelievers among the priests of a certain diocese were often those who in the pulpit and the confessional always "toed the line". What he meant was that precisely those priests whose unbelief was in some respects evident on the surface were the ones who gave no cause for hesitation.

The Necessity of Developing Individual Powers of Belief

Apart from the consideration of the influence of the preacher on the repressed unbelief in those people who are unaware of their repression, one must think of those Christians who "suppress" their unbelief. They sense their lack of belief in some way or other, but usually deal with it by refusing to face up to the fact. Their fear of not being able to believe is not so strong as in the first group of people we have discussed, but it is, nevertheless, an important problem if their faith is to develop.

Such "suppressions" usually appear at certain stages in the development of belief. A new growing or developing stage often will, first of all, manifest itself not as belief but as unbelief. People with these problems find it difficult to understand that any fixed form of belief must of necessity become modified in the course of their lives.

This law of development is not some superfluous luxury, which at best only a few intellectuals can afford to indulge in, but rather a psychological necessity in the life of every man. Whoever is of the opinion that he can (or must) retain until his dying day the form of belief imparted to him in childhood is like the husband who assumes that the image of a wife which he has carried with him since childhood (e.g., the image deriving from his own mother) will enable him to give his own wife her full due for the qualities she possesses in her own right. Adherence to fixed notions, which are meaningful at one stage of development but are no longer adequate in later life, does not of course necessarily lead to dangerous symptoms, but it can lead to conflicts that may have a profound effect in the realm of one's personal beliefs. Such hindrances prevent the deeper and necessary explorations of faith if one is to live a "life that springs from belief".

The phase of unbelief, which frequently heralds a new breakthrough in faith, is only one of many possible manifestations of a situation in which a believer may suppress his faith. There is unfortunately no time to discuss the others in detail here.

Summary

In general the conclusions drawn with regard to the sermon seem to result in the following:—

1. It must have a certain breadth in which the listener can feel free to recognize his own doubts and distress in matters of faith.

2. It must have a depth that will release the listener from the fear that he may "lose" God in his phases of unbelief.

3. It must have a frankness and humility concerning both itself and the Church so that the unbelieving "believer" may feel that the Church is a community in which there is also a place for him.

Vincenzo Miano, S.D.B./*Rome, Italy*

The Tasks Facing the Secretariat for Non-Believers

In the absence of any official document determining the structure and competence of the Secretariat for Non-Believers, I feel bound to say at the outset that this exposition of the tasks facing it is only a modest attempt in order to (1) deduce a few general principles from a number of authoritative texts which refer to it in some sort of way, and (2) to make a provisional summing up of the experience of a little more than a year's existence. The official announcement of the institution of the Secretariat by Pope Paul VI was given in *L'Osservatore Romano* (April 9, 1965), with a brief note to the effect that the Holy Father, in establishing it, had entrusted its presidency to Cardinal König, the Archbishop of Vienna.

I

MOTIVES PROMPTING THE INVITATION TO DIALOGUE

1. *The Mind of the Pope*

In *Ecclesiam suam,* Paul VI seeks to determine "the motives that impel the Church toward dialogue, the methods to be followed and the goals to be achieved". Here the dialogue is understood—and we must draw attention to this—as "a method of accomplishing the apostolic mission", distinguished by the fact "of expressing our teaching with great fairness and explaining it in accordance with the objections of others or despite their slow assimilation of our teaching", and further characterized by its adaptation to the needs of concrete, historic circumstances, both local and individual, without, for all that, ever compromising faithfulness to dogma and moral teaching, or ever falling into irenicism and syncretism. Dialogue stems necessarily and spontaneously from the dogma of the incarnation, because those who bear the message of Christ must share the human condition of those to whom they bear witness, that is, to all men of goodwill, both within and without the Church's own sphere. The Church itself is aware of the "astonishing newness of the modern era", but at the same time remains confident that it possesses a message for all.

The first and the largest of the three concentric circles described by the Pope is truly immense, embracing the whole of the human race, every field where "men are trying to understand themselves and the world". The Church faces up to this universal reality with a heart wide open to the most deepseated aspirations and to the new and sometimes sublime expressions of man's genius. "We are not civilization, but we promote it." Perfect examples of the dialogue of the Church with the modern world are: *Pacem in terris* of John XXIII, of saintly memory, the discourse of Paul VI to the U.N. and the Pastoral *Constitution on the Church in the Modern World*.

In the Church's dialogue with the world, the denial of God is regarded by Paul VI as an obstacle to dialogue, all the more so in that the ideological systems that deny God are often identified with the economic, social and political regimes that oppress the Church, as is precisely the case with atheistic communism. Although in situations like this, dialogue is almost impossible—and in fact gives way to silence—nevertheless, on the part of the Church there are no barriers erected against persons, and for one who loves the truth discussion is always possible.

Along with the declaration and defense of religion, Paul VI

speaks of another important task in regard to atheism: "We are moved by our pastoral office to seek in the heart of the modern atheist the motives of his turmoil and denial. His motives are many and complex, so that we must examine them with care if we are to answer them effectively." He also refers to the distinction drawn by John XXIII between doctrines that remain defined once and for all and the movements issuing from them and which cannot help but evolve and undergo changes, even of a profound nature.

2. Statements of the President of the Secretariat

The Vatican Radio broadcast on April 12, 1965 and the first interviews granted by Cardinal König (KIPA: April 8 and May 15) emphasize the necessity of study and reflection on the phenomenon of contemporary atheism and on the problems that it sets for the Christian religious conscience. The Secretariat in no way intends to organize a crusade, even against militant atheism, but is concerned only with integrating religion into social life and searching out the practical possibilities of dialogue. This naturally presupposes the serious study of the phenomenon of atheism in all its aspects and a knowledge of the various different types of atheism (practical, doctrinaire and militant).

In an interview granted to A. Cavallari of the *Corriere della Sera* (October 24, 1965), during the final period of the Council, Cardinal Konig expressed himself as follows: "Study and knowledge mean understanding and respect. So there will be no conflict with individuals. But understanding and respect do not mean confusion. The objective of the Secretariat is to seek out and to define the limits and the sphere of the dialogue." Participation in conferences and congresses has this precise object; not just a recognition of common values, a kind of dialogue in agreement, but rather study on the problem of man and of religion. Because of the very diversity of situations, this study must be conducted on a regional basis, by means of study groups under the direction of bishops who are members of the Secretariat, with a view to ensure an exchange of information between different parts of the Church. Contemporary atheism is perhaps the most important problem facing the Church today. Dialogue means that we press on in our exploration of the reasons for which man and God appear to be in rivalry with one another, and of why it comes about that man is preferred to God.

3. The Importance of the Decrees of the Council

The *Pastoral Constitution on the Church in the Modern World* is extremely important for the activities of the Secretariat. Paragraphs 19-21 (whose final wording was entrusted to the Secretariat by the Commission) speak of atheism and of the attitude of the Church toward it: "The Church, though she completely rejects atheism, sincerely maintains that all men, believers and unbelievers, should work together to build properly this world in which they live together. This certainly cannot be done without sincere and prudent dialogue." It would appear that in this passage the expression "dialogue" has a different, though related, meaning to that used in *Ecclesiam suam*. By this I mean that it seems to indicate the possibility of collaboration on a human level between believers and unbelievers. The sincerity and prudence, which must characterize the whole dialogue, have as their object to dispel the danger of confusion which is only too real when those taking part, speaking from widely differing standpoints, use the same expressions, but in different senses; and further, to avoid the danger of making the dialogue instrumental in furthering ends that are quite foreign to it.

4. The Practical Obligations of the Secretariat

To conclude this first section, it seems that we can draw the following conclusions as to the tasks facing the Secretariat:

(a) The Secretariat must promote the knowledge and the study of the various forms of unbelief. (This expression can be interpreted in the sense of either systematic atheism or agnosticism and *de facto* indifferentism to the whole question of God, so much so that if we do understand it in this way, all those who do not adhere to some religion, either as a matter of conviction or as a pattern of life, are to be classified as unbelievers.) The study to be encouraged by the Secretariat is intended to seek out and identify the deep underlying motives prompting indifference, doubt and the denial of God, and will, therefore, be not only historico-doctrinal but also of a psycho-sociological nature.

(b) On the other hand, the Secretariat must promote theological and pastoral reflection in order to ensure that the presentation of Christianity corresponds to the aspirations present in contemporary atheism, in the light of experiments that are taking place in this field.

(c) It must bring to the attention of the pastors and faithful in the Church the outcome and the conclusions drawn from this study and reflection, as well as those derived from pastoral experiments.

(d) It must seek to ascertain the practical possibilities of a dialogue between organized groups with the intention, in the first place, of bringing about a confrontation in the doctrinal field, which will be without controversy, designed to eliminate prejudice and to promote a more fruitful mutual understanding; then, secondly, through the careful search for common grounds of agreement on a human level where this is possible, without confusion or cross purposes, to pave the way for collaboration between believers and unbelievers for the construction of a better world.

II

PROGRESS REALIZED IN WORK UNDERTAKEN TO DATE

1. *Basic Structures*

How has the Secretariat attempted to achieve these objectives? First of all, a minimum of organization had to be provided. It was decided at the outset that the central feature of the organization, around which all else revolved, would be a group of bishops, who, taken together, would represent different parts of the Church: individual conferences or a small number of episcopal conferences of similar nature drawn from neighboring regions. In the course of the last session of the Council, at the suggestion of the President who had consulted the heads of the episcopal conferences, 23 bishops (now 24) were nominated by the Holy Father, with the prior knowledge of the Secretariat of State. These, together with the President, constitute the *deliberative assembly,* and the first meetings took place during the final days of the Council. The episcopal members of the Secretariat have also the duty of maintaining contact with the episcopates of the various countries, and of setting up and pre-siding—in person, or through a reliable representative—over *teams* of specialists and scholars, which, in fact, could almost be described as local secretariats.

The principal collaborators with the bishops are the *con-sultors.* Up to the present moment more than 50 have been nominated by the Holy Father, and these were chosen with an eye both to the competence of their knowledge and to their being representative of different backgrounds and countries: thus, most of them reside outside Rome. The bishops have the power to choose other collaborators and to seek assistance from the universities and other learned and pastoral institutes. Ac-cording to the size of various countries, there can be more than one of these groups and centers.

The nomination of a number of *non-Catholic consultors* is also foreseen. In any case, fraternal collaboration with the other Christian Churches and Communities has been initiated aus-piciously both locally and on a worldwide basis. Thus, contacts have been established both with the World Council of Churches at Geneva and with a number of confessional groups, for it is a fact that the whole range of the problems presented today by atheism and laicism (secularization) is common to all Christians, and indeed to all men sincerely concerned about the future of religious values.

2. *Present Activities*

The central Secretariat (consisting of the general Secretariat and a number of consultors) has also sought to establish direct contact with the Catholic universities and higher institutes by sending them a *questionnaire* for the purpose of obtaining information as to what studies have up to the present been devoted to this problem and what future plans have been made regarding this. As a result, the intention in the future is to promote a higher degree of collaboration between men engaged in Catholic scholarship. In particular, the ground has been explored for the establishment at Rome of a center of studies on contemporary atheism in conjunction with the ecclesiastical universities. In general, through contact with the Sacred Congregation of Seminaries and Universities, the Secretariat intends to see that in the renewal of ecclesiastical studies the problem of modern atheism is kept well to the fore. With the intention of facilitating a mutual exchange of information between different parts of the Church, the Secretariat has started to publish a *Bulletin* (for the moment, mimeographed) containing a number of selected studies, along with news and reports of congresses, etc. An international review giving facilities for dialogue with unbelievers themselves is also much to be desired. The Bulletin is sent to the member bishops, presidents and secretaries of the episcopal conferences, consultors and other collaborators. In regard to promoting the dialogue, the Secretariat has accepted the *invitations* addressed to it to assist through an observer, or to participate with its representatives, at international study meetings between groups of believers and non-believers. When the occasion arises, it will also be able to organize similar gatherings itself. But its main effort, with the cooperation of its own experts, is directed to the study of the theological foundations, the various forms and principles of the dialogue, with a view to its fruitful development and the furthering of its immediate and remote objectives. It is clear that the dialogue, viewed in its broadest implications, is the work of the whole Church and of each Christian according to his individual responsibilities. The task of the Secretariat is to see to it that the dialogue is directed to its proper ends. It has no competence to involve itself in projects of a strictly temporal nature.

As stated above, we are still at the experimental stage, and the tasks I have outlined as being at present incumbent on the Secretariat can, as opportunity allows, be adjusted or developed further—*usus docebit*.

PART II
BIBLIOGRAPHICAL
SURVEY

Erwin Adler / *Munich, West Germany*

Basic Tendencies in the Atheistic Propaganda Literature

INTRODUCTION

The importance of the atheistic and anti-religious literature of the Eastern block should not be underestimated. The political and economic system of those States that are committed to the communist goal is founded on a materialistic philosophy. The philosophical basis of communism is the philosophy of Marxism-Leninism, dialectical and historical materialism. As a consciously materialistic philosophy, Marxism-Leninism is in conflict with religion, which rejects a purely materialistic interpretation of the world and human society. This opposition between Marxist-Leninist philosophy and religion is expressed in the large amount of atheistic and anti-religious literature in the Eastern block.

In this survey we shall consider only the atheistic and anti-religious literature of the Soviet Union, since the other Eastern block States have scarcely any important original contributions to offer in this field; generally, they use only translations from Russian.

The first part of the survey is concerned with the most important representatives of Soviet atheism and their works, the basic textbooks on the questions of atheism and the criticism of religion, reference works and atheistic periodicals. The second part is devoted to an account of the main lines of Soviet atheistic and anti-religious, anti-Christian and anti-Church propaganda literature. Finally, the third section endeavors to make a critical contribution to the problem of Eastern atheism.

I

EASTERN ATHEISM AS SEEN IN ITS MAIN REPRESENTATIVES AND IN THE ANTI-RELIGIOUS WRITING OF THE EAST

In the mere half century of its existence, the atheistic and anti-religious, anti-Christian and anti-Church literature of the Eastern block has assumed unimaginable proportions. Eastern readers have been, and still are, overwhelmed by a great flood of propaganda brochures, newspaper articles and longer works. Atheistic and anti-religious, anti-Christian and anti-Church literature in the East already fills whole libraries. Here we shall discuss only those authors and works or periodicals which are of some importance.

PLECHANOV

The leading Marxist of Russia is considered to be Georgii Valentinovitch Plechanov. In his large literary output he did not restrict himself solely to questions of philosophy and the science of history, but he was also concerned in some detail with the phenomenon of religion. His writings that criticize religion still enjoy today great popularity in the Soviet Union, as is shown by the publication of large new editions.

As a Marxist, Plechanov was also consciously a materialist, and as such, logically, an atheist. Religion is for him a form of social awareness, a reflection of social life. Man fashions his religious ideas on the model of the social order he finds about him. They have no truth content. Religion is a "product of false conception of nature and of society".[1] It is closely connected with animism, both in origin and in its most evolved and highest forms. For Plechanov there is no form of religion that does not show traces of animism.[2] Religion is "belief in spiritual beings who exist alongside physical things and the processes of nature".[3]

---

[1] Note: There are unfortunately no German, French or English translations of the majority of the works cited. Plechanov, *O religii i cerkvi* (Moscow, 1957), p. 73. (*Concerning Religion and the Church*).

[2] *Cf. ibid.*, p. 294.

[3] *Ibid.*, p. 152.

With the aid of this animistic belief man endeavors to explain all the mysterious processes of nature. At a higher level this primitive animistic element is joined by another moral one, so that religion is then seen as a belief in spiritual beings that is connected with morality and sanctions it.

The origin of the idea of God as the center-piece of religion is also explained by Plechanov from an animistic point of view. Primitive man began to concern himself with the phenomena of his inner life. Because of his experience of dreams, the events of the loss of consciousness and of death, he came to think that in his body there lived a soul which could not be known by the senses. From this idea of the soul he later moved on to the acceptance of the existence of non-material spiritual beings that can be found in nature alongside material bodies and are active in it. These spiritual beings then became gods. With the growth in power of a few men who first appear as leaders and then as rulers of the community, the idea of God grows in importance. The gods demand sacrifices, issue commandments and are seen as the judges of humanity. Finally, the idea of God comes to dominate the thinking and actions of men so much that their whole life is subject to the inescapable influence of the idea of God. God appears as the omnipotent creator and lord of all nature, men and spirits, and he also exercises over all an unrestricted office as judge.

According to Plechanov there is a close connection between religious ideas and economic and social life. Influenced by the economic conditions of human life and the change and development in economic conditions, social life also changes and develops, and with it the religious ideas of men. When man stood helpless facing nature, he regarded the other living things as higher and more powerful than himself and ascribed divine qualities to them, and thus totemism developed. In the later epochs of his history, however, when he learned to resist nature and to harness its forces, he freed himself from his totemistic ideas and no longer regarded animals as higher beings, but began to use them as providers of food or as tools of work. In this way, man's power over nature increased still further. In harmony with this, he altered his idea of God to correspond to his own image—he anthropomorphized it. Totemism is replaced by anthropomorphic gods in accordance with the economic changes.

Plechanov regards religion and the idea of God as having a reactionary social role in human history. Religion sanctions the existing differences in wealth; it supports, or even causes, the division of human society into castes and classes and threatens those individuals or groups that rebel against social injustice with the most severe punishments in the next life. For this reason, religion is often an insuperable obstacle in the way of every social revolution and all social progress. Plechanov holds that many priests of many religions who do not themselves believe in God want to preserve religious faith among the people only because they see in it a support for the governing classes who reward them for it, or at least they consider it a necessary element of all social order. Here Plechanov directs his attack especially against Christian spirituality, which in his view has played an almost exclusively reactionary role in the history of Europe.

LUNATCHARSKI

The Marxist philosopher, poet and politician, Anatol Lunatcharski, occupied a curious position among the Eastern critics of religion. Together with other Russian Marxists he held that socialism must not fight religion, but make an alliance with it. In studying the historical bases of Marxism, Lunatcharski was deeply impressed by the sublime ideas of the German idealists, especially by their views on religion. He found only a negative attitude to religious questions in the materialist thinkers. Thus, he set about revising the attitude of scientific socialism to religion. He confronted Marxism with religion and tried to show the features that they had in common. For Lunatcharski, religion is a complex of thought and feeling that is a psychological solution of the tension between the laws of life and the laws of nature.[4] It is a living phenomenon that never dies out, but continually progresses from one stage to the next. Scientific socialism, which resolves the opposition between the laws of nature and laws of life by proclaiming the victory of life over nature, the subjugation of the forces of nature by reason, is thus equally religion, indeed it is the "last, profoundly critical, purified and, at the same time, synthetic religious system".[5]

Religion comes into existence in man together with his awareness of his own incompleteness, with his awareness of the opposition between life and nature, between the ideal and reality. Man strives to preserve his life. Since he cannot attain this goal as a weak individual, he conceives the idea of the presence of supernatural beings not subject to nature. Thus arose the belief in spirits and gods and the belief in the immortality of the individual, as the supra-individual element of religion. Modern man no longer believes in spirits and gods, but only in the reality that can be known through the senses. But experience tells us of two supra-individual entities, the world and humanity, and these two entities now constitute the supra-individual part of the new religion, the religion of socialism. Socialism places the species higher than the individual; in this way it multiplies the powers of individuals. For this reason socialism is a higher kind of religion. Socialism requires that man give meaning to the world. It contains an element that is new from the religious point of view: hope, hope for the victory of mankind in the fight with nature.

As a Marxist Lunatcharski considers that the religious ideas of men develop according to the economic and social situation of society. In the early human community the gods were only one's dead relatives or members of the tribe. When leaders and rulers later emerged and the social structure changed, the gods also acquired the qualities of rulers. When aristocratic

[4] Lunatcharski, *Religija i socialism* (Petersburg, 1908), p. 40. (*Religion and Socialism*).
[5] *Ibid.*, II, p. 213.

rule succeeded tyrannical rule, followed by the democratic form of society, the gods also assumed more humane characteristics.

In the priestly caste, Lunatcharski sees the institutional, conservative element of religion, whereas the prophets are the embodiment of progress. The true prophets have always opposed the reactionary elements of society and called the masses to fight them. From Zarathustra and Moses to the present day, they show humanity the way of truth. They sacrificed their own happiness to the happiness of mankind and thus showed themselves the proclaimers of a true religiosity, since this consists in going beyond oneself. Lunatcharski sees the greatest of all prophets as the founder of scientific socialism, Karl Marx. In his opinion, he was the one who showed mankind the true way to happiness.

Lunatcharski admires the old forms of religion for their beauty. He favors the acceptance of its glorious myths, which are only an expression of the eternal struggle of mankind with nature, through the new religion of socialism. Christ, for example, is for Lunatcharski the divinized working man, human work made into a god. It is the same with the myth of Prometheus and Heracles.

These ideas of Lunatcharski had a strong influence on the Russian Marxists. There arose among them the movement of the so-called "God-makers", who endeavored to reconcile Marxism with religion, even to turn Marxism itself into a religion. The God of the new religion, the religion of scientific socialism, had to be created (hence that name, in contrast to the movement of the so-called "God-seekers" in Russia). The celebrated writer, Maxim Gorki, was also one of them.

LENIN

Vladimir Iliitch Lenin opposed the attempts of the God-makers. He devoted a number of essays to the questions of religion and referred to these problems in his philosophical writings also. For him, as for Marx and Plechanov, religion is not an independent phenomenon, but is inseparably bound up with the economic conditions of society. It is without any objective basis, merely a product of the human imagination, and, as such, is only "jejune idealistic nonsense".[6] It owes its origin to man's helplessness. With the primitive man of early times the root of the origin of religion lay in his struggle with unfriendly nature. With the proletariat, however, that is exploited by the capitalist economic system; capital, and the struggle against capital, have engendered religious ideas in the human consciousness. Religion is "a kind of spiritual pressure which everywhere and in every sphere weighs on the masses, who are demoralized by eternally working for others, by suffering and loneliness. Therefore, the helplessness in the struggle against the exploiters inevitably creates belief in a better life beyond the grave, just as the helplessness of the savage in his fight with nature engenders belief in gods, devils, miracles, etc." [7] Religion is the opium of the people, a kind of spiritual alcohol, a "purified, refined poison for the oppressed masses".[8] Thus, there can be no reconciliation between scientific socialism and religion for Lenin. In contrast to Lunatcharski and his supporters, Lenin cannot see anything of value in the idea of God.

In his letters to Maxim Gorki (Gorki was at that time one of the so-called God-makers and wrote his story, *The Confession,* under the influence of the ideas of this movement), he even describes the idea of God as necrophilia. "To speak of the search for God, not in order to oppose all gods and devils, all spiritual necrophilia (every god means necrophilia; even if it is the purest, most ideal, not sought but created god, it doesn't matter), but in order to prefer a blue devil to a yellow one, is a hundred times worse than not speaking about it at all." [9] The newly constructed, pure idea of God is far more dangerous for Lenin than the crude ideas of God found in primitive religions, since it is easier to unmask these, fight them and make them harmless to the people. "A Catholic priest who rapes

[6] Lenin, *Sotchinenia* (Moscow, 1941-60, Vol. 38), p. 305. (*Works*)
[7] *Ibid.,* Vol. 10, p. 65.
[8] *Ibid.,* Vol. 16, p. 295.
[9] *Ibid.,* Vol. 35, p. 89.

girls . . . is far less dangerous for 'democracy' than a priest without vestments, a priest without crude religion, a priest who is democratic and filled with an idea and who preaches the creation of a God. For it is easy to unmask, condemn and get rid of the first priest, but you cannot get rid of the second one so easily; it is a thousand times more difficult to unmask him; there won't be any 'sickly and self-pitying' *petit bourgeois* who will be ready to condemn him." [10] For Lenin, God is only a complex of ideas that came into being as a result of the oppression of man by external nature and class tyranny; and these ideas make this oppression even more firmly entrenched and dull the edge of the class struggle.

Under the influence of Lenin's attacks, Lunatcharski gave up his "God-making" endeavors, and Gorki did the same. Lunatcharski accepted Lenin's viewpoint on the religious question and also adopted an unfriendly attitude to religion from then on. After the victory of the Bolsheviks he became the people's commissar for enlightenment (minister of education) in the first Soviet government. In his writings on the science of religion, he adopted the official Marxist-Leninist position.

Lenin did not concern himself only theoretically with the phenomenon of religion, but he also determined the attitude of the Party and of the State to it. The State must take a neutral stand in relation to religion (which naturally involves the complete separation of State and Church), but the Party, as a fighting group, which is committed to the philosophy of dialectical and historical materialism, cannot be neutral to religion, but must endeavor to educate the broad masses of the people in the spirit of atheism and to remove all the remaining vestiges of religious belief in stages, by enlightenment and scientific propaganda (this idea of Lenin also influenced the Soviet constitution).

JAROSLAVSKI

Emilian Jaroslavski is one of the chief representatives of Soviet atheism and the Soviet criticism of religion. Even before the

[10] *Ibid.*, Vol. 3, p. 90.

October Revolution he wrote various works in the struggle against religion. In his *Soldier's Catechism* he described religion as the ally of those who wielded political power. Belief in God only serves to persuade the uneducated man that all authority must be acknowledged and tolerated, since it comes from God. The chief motive of all wars, even religious ones, is not the service of God, but the naked desire for power and possession. After the October Revolution Jaroslavski founded the Society of the Godless Militants of the U.S.S.R. and became chairman of this society. As the editor of the periodicals *Besboshnik* (*The Man without God*) and *Antireligiosnik* (*The Antireligious Man*), he wrote a number of essays and treatises that were atheistic and critical of religion. On his initiative the Central Museum of the History of Religion was founded in Moscow, which was later transferred to Leningrad under the name of the Museum of the History of Religion and Atheism.

Jaroslavski saw religious institutions, churches and monastic communities as the determined opponents of the communist social system. In the Soviet Union they have, he thinks, succumbed under the pressure of events to the power of the working class and are loyal to the Soviet power, whereas in the non-communist countries they openly oppose socialism. They abuse the religious ideas and feelings of the population, in order to prepare, with the aid of religion, a new crusade against the Soviet Union. In his essay, "How gods and goddesses are born, live and die", he endeavors to present religion in the form of the comparative history of religion and to divest it of its supernatural contents. All religious ideas have been created by men themselves, all the gods have been born from men themselves. Under the same or similar conditions, the same or similar religious ideas and religious practices grew up among the different peoples. The figure of the mother of God, the virgin birth, the Son of God, the resurrection, the trinity—all these Jaroslavski regards as religious myths, the motifs of which occur in many religions, and are even dependent on one another. In his work, *The Bible for Believers and Unbelievers,* Jaroslavski attempts to reduce the Old and New Testaments to a purely human origin. The bible represents a collection of writings written in various times by various authors; it is only a compilation of the traditions and legends of the Jewish people and its neighbors. The contents of the books of scripture contradict the knowledge discovered by the historical and natural sciences. An enlightened modern man cannot take the bible as the Word of God.

BONTCH-BRUYEVITCH

Another critic of religion, Vladimir Bontch-Bruyevitch, concerned himself particularly with the history of religious movements in Russia. He was interested, above all, in the connection between the religious social movements and the political class struggle. He tried to enlist the aid of the Russian sects for the Revolution and took the view that religious movements in Russia are basically only an expression of the class differences and the class struggle. They must, therefore, be specially noted, since they could be a help to the Party. Thus, under the influence of Bontch-Bruyevitch the Party issued a special periodical with the name *Rassvet*, which not only disseminated social and political ideas among religious groups, but made a cautious attempt to supplant religion and belief in God. The bible became the object of critical treatment, and Christianity and the authority of the Gospels systematically and skilfully undermined. The origin of religion was explained to the readers as a natural phenomenon. The Party sympathized with the religious social movements, but not with the philosophical basis of these movements.

Systematic Textbooks of Atheism

Soviet atheistic and anti-religious literature is not limited only to the works of the more important atheists we have discussed, but it also contains a number of systematic textbooks that are devoted to the questions of atheism and the critique of religion. For example, the Institute of Philosophy at the U.S.S.R. Academy of Sciences published a textbook with the title *Osnovy nautchnogo ateisma* (*The Elements of Scientific Atheism*), which attempts to give a systematic explanation of the nature of religion, its origin and its particular historical forms, as well as the nature of atheism, from the standpoint of Marxism-Leninism. Religion and its beliefs are sharply criticized, and atheism contrasted with the world of religious faith as a "system of materialistic, scientifically founded views which reject belief in God or gods, supernatural powers or any religion".[11] In all important questions, religion contradicts scientific knowledge: in its conception of nature and its processes, in its views on the origin, the nature and the goal of human life, its view of human society, the State and history. The textbook deals with what it calls the unscientific bourgeois theories on the origin of religion and belief in God and tries to show the reader that only atheism, especially Marxist atheism, can give a scientific answer to the chief questions of life. Atheism is as old as religion. When religion first appeared some men doubted its truth, and hence, as a result of this doubt, atheism was born. In the course of its history it has taken various forms. But only Marxist atheism, which is based on the newest discoveries of science, gives a satisfactory answer to the questions connected with the phenomenon of religion. For modern man, religion can have no further attraction, both because it is unscientific and also because of its false religious morality; communist morality and religious morality are irreconcilably opposed. Hence, the communist party is concerned to fight all the vestiges that still remain of religious ideas and to remove them from the life of society. But this goal requires, above all, intensively conducted atheistic and anti-religious propaganda, which enlists the aid of modern science in its struggle against religion.

Another important atheistic and anti-religious textbook is the work, *Sputnik ateista* (*The Atheist's Companion*). In separate chapters, it deals with the origin of religion, the main types of religion (Hinduism, Buddhism, Taoism, Confucianism, Judaism, Christianity in its various branches, and Islam), the sacred writ-

[11] *Osnovy nautchnogo ateisma* (Moscow, 1962), p. 3.

ings of religions, religious festivals and customs, the relation between religion and modern science, between religious morality
and communist morality, and the relation of the communist State
and the communist party to religion and to the Churches. In its
last section, the book attempts to make the contents of the previous chapters more vivid by the use of illustrations. There are
descriptions of the ideas of the next world held by savages:
their magic practices are described, the myths and gods of the
various religions are presented by means of pictures and photo-
graphs and the negative function of the Christian Churches and
of Christian spirituality illustrated (the burning of heretics, the
torture chambers of the Inquisition, bishops and ministers blessing weapons and warriors).

In 1964, the Institute of Philosophy at the U.S.S.R. Academy
of Sciences published a *Scientific Atheist Dictionary*, which
treated in alphabetical order the most important religious and
theological ideas, as well as a number of figures who have played
an important part in the history of religions and atheism. For
the authors of this reference book God is, for example, "the
illusory chief object of faith and worship in all religions . . .
The idea of God represents the fantastic image of a supernatural
being who has a power unattainable by men, of which it can
make use to their advantage or disadvantage".[12] Religious dogmas are "fantastic assertions about God made by those who foster
his cult and other religious ideas that contradict the whole of
man's experience of life and science, but are declared to be ir-
refutable "truths revealed by God, whose meaning is beyond
the understanding of men".[13] Under the heading "Thomas
Aquinas" we find the statement that this theologian "opposed
the progressive ideas of his time. By defending the interests of
the ruling classes he elaborated the Christian doctrine of the
world, an hierarchic system fixed for all times, and of God, who
sanctions the power of the monarch on earth, social inequality
and the feudal yoke".[14]

[12] *Kratkid nautschno-ateistitcheskik slovar* (Moscow, 1964), p. 76.
[13] *Ibid.*, p. 175.
[14] *Ibid.*, p. 571f.

Periodicals

There are also anti-religious periodicals that serve atheistic propaganda; they appear in large editions and always carry short articles on religious and Church subjects. Among the best known of these periodicals are *Voprosy istorii religii i ateisma* (*Questions of the History of Religion and of Atheism*), *Yeshegodnik musea istorii religii i ateisma* (*Annual of the Museum of the History of Religion and of Atheism*), and *Nauka i religia* (*Science and Religion*). *Questions of the History of Religion and of Atheism* is published by the U.S.S.R. Academy of Sciences and has appeared as a monthly since 1954. As its title suggests, it is devoted primarily to subjects from the history of religion: to the history of individual religions, religious movements and sects, and the life and works of the better-known representatives of atheism and the criticism of religion. The *Annual of the Museum of the History of Religion and of Atheism* has also been published since 1957 by the Academy of Sciences and prints more systematic treatises on the science of religion as well as essays on the history of religion. The periodical, *Science and Religion,* has more a popular science quality and has appeared as a monthly since January, 1960.

Philosophical Textbooks

The propaganda of atheism and of the criticism of religion and the Churches is treated in the Eastern block only by purely technical writings, but there are also the textbooks of Marxist-Leninist philosophy and the philosophical and general reference books that serve this purpose. The well-known *Elements of Marxist Philosophy* (*Osnovy marksistskoi filosofii*), compiled by a number of philosophers, published by the Institute of Philosophy in the U.S.S.R. Academy of Sciences in several editions, and disseminated through all the States of the Eastern block, gives a materialistic, atheistic world view. All of reality consists of one principle only, matter; mind and consciousness are only a function of matter. A principle outside or above the world is completely rejected. God is only a product of the human imagination. Religion is a part of the ideological superstructure of the particular form of society and will die away in the course of the realization of the classless society.

It is the same with the other textbooks of Marxist philosophy (cf., for example, B. A. Spirkin's *Course of Marxist Philosophy*,[15] D. Tchesnokov's *Historical Materialism*,[16] the textbook, *Marxist-Leninist Philosophy*,[17] etc.). The philosophical encyclopaedias also make atheistic and anti-religious propaganda. The edition of the *Filosofskaia entsiklopedia* (*Philosophical Encyclopaedia*) in several volumes, which the Institute of Philosophy at the Academy of Sciences began publishing in 1960, describes God as a "fantastic image that is at the basis of every belief and expresses the idea of a supernatural being who has a particular power".[18] Jesus is a legendary figure, the "mythical founder of Christianity".[19] Even the general works of reference, for example, the fifty-volume *Bolshaia Sovietskaia entsiklopedia* (*Great Soviet Encyclopaedia*) is full of atheistic ideas, and religion is described in it as a "distorted, fantastic reflection in the human mind of the forces of nature and society that dominate man";[20] God is a "mythical, fictitious being";[21] Christianity is a "fantastic, perverse reflection of the social structure which has an historically transient character.[22]

II

THE BASIC LINES OF THE ATHEISTIC AND ANTI-CHURCH PROPAGANDA LITERATURE IN THE EASTERN BLOCK

After reviewing the main representatives of Soviet atheism and the most important works of Soviet atheistic and anti-religious

[15] *Kurs marksistskoj filosofii* (Moscow, 1964).

[16] *Istoritcheskij materialism* (Moscow, 1965).

[17] *Marksistako-leninskaia filosofia* (Moscow, 1965).

[18] Vol. 1, p. 175.

[19] Vol. II. p. 249.

[20] *Bolshaia Sovietskaia entsiklopedia* (Moscow, 1949 et seq., Vol. 36, p. 335.

[21] *Ibid.*, Vol. 5, p. 336.

[22] *Ibid.*, Vol. 46, p. 352.

propaganda literature, we shall try to present a systematic summary of the foundations of atheistic and anti-religious literature in the Eastern block.

The Systematic Structure of Eastern Atheism

Eastern atheism is based primarily on the atheistic ideas and anti-religious writings of Karl Marx and Friedrich Engels, and, beyond these, on the critique of religion given by neo-Hegelianism in Germany. But Soviet atheism is based also on a special Russian tradition. Eastern atheism was introduced especially by the so-called Russian revolutionary democrats and their writings, critical of religion and opposed to the Church. In comparison with Marxist atheism it is much more radical (cf., e.g., the attacks by Lenin against religion and the belief in God). In the course of the last decades it assumed an essentially more unified and systematic form. Because of the fact that Eastern Europe has been dominated for decades by the Marxist-Leninist philosophy, Soviet atheism has a longer experience in its struggle with religion and the Churches.

Eastern atheism is an essential ingredient of the Marxist-Leninist philosophy of dialectical and historical materialism. Dialectical materialism, i.e., the ontology, natural philosophy and epistemology of Marxism-Leninism, teaches that the whole universe, in fact, the whole sphere of being is of a material nature. Only matter and its movement exist. Consciousness is not set against matter as an independent principle, but as a product, a function of the matter that is best and most highly organized: the human brain. There is no place in this philosophy for God and an immortal human soul.

Historical materialism, i.e., the conception of history and society, the Marxist-Leninist philosophy of the State and of law, is also concerned with the phenomenon of religion. It starts from the doctrine of the basis and the superstructure of society. Historical materialism regards economic circumstances as the so-called basis of society; all political, legal and ideological ideas and the institutions that correspond to them (the State, law, morality, art, philosophy, religion, the Churches, etc.), as the superstructure. The superstructure of society is conditioned by the economic structure of society; it depends on it. The superstructure is nothing but the reflection of the economic structure of society. All the changes in the superstructure have their origin in the changes of the economic structure. Every form of society has its own basis and its own superstructure. The social superstructure reflects the relationships between the classes.

The Polemical Attitude to Religion

Religion is one of the forms of the social superstructure. It is a distorted reflection in the human brain of nature and of social relationships. No objective reality corresponds to it. It is used by the dominating classes for the spiritual and hence also political and economic enslavement, of the working masses. Since it promises to the oppressed an eternal happiness in the next world, it reconciles them to the earthly domination of the oppressors and exploiters, by inducing humility and obedience in the workers, and in this way, distracting interest from the fight for liberation. Religious institutions, especially the Christian Churches, always furthered social oppression. For example, the Churches recognized slavery and serfdom and represented them as a divine institution. Any revolutionary who opposed these inhuman institutions was excommunicated. The popes represent capitalism in their social encyclicals as an expression of the divine will and order the workers to accept the place where God has put them without murmuring. All believers who fight with communism against the exploitation of the masses are threatened with exclusion from the community of the Church. The greatest and most important of all religious communities, the Catholic Church and its spiritual and political center, the Vatican, is only a "limited company for the intellectual enslavement and exploitation of many peoples".[23] It supported and still supports fascist governments and with the aid of the Christian parties it pursues a policy that is directed against the real interests of the poorer

[23] *Osnovy markistskoi filosofii*, p. 568.

sections of the people. The Russian Orthodox Church was just the same; it supported the Czars and the feudal lords. During and after the October Revolution, it was the ally of the counter-revolutionary forces. Equally, the Protestant Churches are wholly dependent on the particular rule of the country.

But religion and its institutions are not only a reactionary reality, from the social and political viewpoint, but they also contradict science. Religion and its representatives fought constantly in history against scientific knowledge and against all the innovations that are based on this knowledge. They forbade free thought to man and sought in this way to enslave him mentally. Representatives of science, who would not give in to superstition, were tortured and executed by the representatives of the Churches. The Churches' opposition to science lasts until the present day.

According to the Marxist view religion did not always exist. The first men did not have any religion and did not believe in God. It was only at a particular stage of development that religious ideas arose in the human consciousness and, in common with these, also religious cults. The first forms of religion were the animistic and totemistic cults. Later, through personification and anthropomorphization, different deities arose, and finally, the monotheistic religions came into being.

The Call to Fight Religion

The central idea of all religions, that of God, is for the Soviet Marxist not innate and not a revealed object of belief, but a product of the imagination of ignorant, primitive man, to which no objective reality corresponds. It came about because of the anxiety of primitive, helpless man when faced with the unknown, to him mysterious, powers of nature. With scientific enlightenment and with the domination of the forces of nature by human reason, and, above all, with the common fight of man against nature and the growing power of the individual through the collective, the realization of socialism, which does away with the dependence of one man upon another and mutual exploitation, the basis of the belief in God disappears, namely, the helplessness and ignorance of man. Thus, in the epoch of socialism the belief in God will yield its place to an atheistic view of the world and die out.

But the Soviet Marxists do not rely on the tendency of religion and the belief in God to die out as a result of historical and social development. In order to accelerate the process of the disappearance of religion (and this process must be accelerated, since religion and belief in God exercise a reactionary function that hinders the building of the classless communist society), all forms of religious faith must be fiercely opposed. This fight, although it must be ruthless, is not to be carried on administratively, not by the use of force by the police or by persecution, but on the basis of ideological debate and of convincing people. To this end there is atheistic education of children and young people in school; atheistic and anti-religious propaganda in public life; atheistic literature, anti-religious exhibitions and films. In the faculties of arts of Soviet universities, chairs for atheism have been set up; in the large towns and former religious centers, atheistic and anti-religious museums were founded (as, for example, the atheistic museum in the former monastery in a cave at Kiev, the Museum of the History of Religion and Atheism in a former cathedral in Leningrad); publishing houses and newspaper editors overwhelm their readers with long anti-religious treatises and shorter pamphlets in which religion is ridiculed in the eyes of those who still believe.

The more important atheistic writings of the past and the anti-religious works from foreign countries are translated and republished. But religious institutions are penalized from the start in this ideological warfare. The radical separation of Church and State and of Church and the schools was carried out radically. Children and youth are given the necessary knowledge within the framework of an atheistic view of the world, and the representatives of the Churches are not allowed to go to the schools. The publishing activity of the religious groups is reduced to a minimum. In other words, the population is exposed to intensive

atheistic propaganda and has almost no chance of informing itself concerning religion objectively from independent sources.
(Poland is an exception here: despite intensive atheistic and
anti-religious State propaganda, despite atheistic societies, whose
function exists exclusively in combating religious faith in people
by the publication of anti-religious periodicals and treatises, the
Church has several publishing houses and periodicals. The Polish
communists have tried and still try to soften up the unified
"block" of believers by supporting groups of so-called "progressive" Catholics and priests, who seek to bring about a positive
attitude to communism in the population.)

III

A CRITICAL CONTRIBUTION TO THE PROBLEM
OF EASTERN ATHEISM

The Christian, like the religious man in general, is amazed
that in Eastern Europe—a geographical area where religion and
the Church had an important influence for centuries, where religion was probably the central concern of the population—sud-
denly there has arisen an atheistic and anti-religious movement
which is unprecedented in history, the waves of which overwhelm everything and seriously threaten the existence of religion
and the Church. Russia, in particular, was especially rich in
religious traditions. Throughout that vast country, churches and
monasteries flourished; holy places attracted pious pilgrims from
every region; the population was profoundly influenced by religion and by Christianity; the government was not only friendly
to the Church, but supported its endeavors to the highest degree.
People even spoke of "Holy Russia".

The Unity of the Throne and the Altar
in the Czarist Empire

In order to understand the change that has taken place in the
20th century, we must go back a little further into the history

of Russia. The Church had a powerful influence on the life of
the people and of the State, but this influence was too powerful.
The Church was in too narrow an alliance with the State; probably nowhere in Europe was the connection between the throne
and the altar, of secular power and religious authority, so close
as in Russia. Since Peter I, the Czar was equally the head of the
Church (the patriarchate was no longer occupied), and the
Orthodox Church was the strongest support of the power of the
Czars. And this power of the Czar was exercised in the history
of the Russian people in an unimaginably cruel way. For the
slightest criticism of the regime there were the severest penalties,
and many of the finest sons of Russia had to languish in exile
or were executed. Any rebellion against the Czar was considered
as a rebellion against God.

As a result of this Caesaropapism, many people from the
educated classes turned away from the Church. A large movement of criticism arose that was at first anti-clerical, then anti-
Christian, and finally, anti-religious and atheistic, a current that
was also augmented from Western sources (especially by the
French enlightenment and German materialism). Because of the
close connection between Church and State, the revolutionary
movements were directed also against religion. The Russian revo-
lutionaries saw in religion only a spiritual prop of the hated
Czarist regime and thus sought to destroy it. After the fall of
the Czarist regime they set about fulfilling these aims.

The Structural Weaknesses of the Eastern Church

Apart from the very narrow links between the Church and
the secular power, the specific character of Orthodox piety also
played a big part. The contemplative side of religious life was
overemphasized, and the active life too much neglected. The
social question which the Churches in Western Europe had long
taken note of and come to grips with, was almost completely
ignored in the Orthodox Church.

Nor was the Russian Church particularly noted for the great
learnedness of its representatives. The theological and general

training of the Orthodox clergy had many gaps. Whereas there was much publishing activity in the Western Churches, not limited solely to liturgical and biblical books, but more or less including also apologetic, philosophical and even belles lettres, the Eastern Church was hardly prepared to face the critical attacks on religion.

The representatives of Russian religious criticism and of Russian (and later Soviet) atheism also had had unfortunate experiences with the representatives of the Church. A number of them had studied theology. Their negative personal experiences contributed greatly to their later fierce opposition to the Church and religion.

What Is False in the Criticism of Religion in the East

Therefore, the representatives of religion and of the Church deserve a large share of the blame for the rise and spread of Eastern atheism. But that does not mean that the other side is wholly right in its attacks on religion. On the one hand, it is true that the Churches often let themselves be misused in the course of history for base ends, and representatives of the Churches and religious communities used the religious convictions of the faithful in order to attain political or economic ends that scarcely had anything in common with religion or morality. On the other hand, the Eastern atheists and critics of religion have also been guilty of great exaggerations. In their writings on religious questions, they use arguments that are not only, for the most part, out of date, because they go back to Marx and Engels and thus to a time in which the criticism of religion was still at a rather primitive level, but they also crudely distort the nature of religion itself. Hardly anyone will question that, for example, in both the past and the present, religion was and is misused by various people for disreputable ends, and thus has exercised a negative function. But the positive contributions of religion should, in justice, not be overlooked. The Eastern atheists write extensively concerning the negative incidental phenomena of religious life, the persecution of heretics by the Churches, the trials of the Inquisition and of witches, religious wars and crusades, the support of the rulers by the representatives of religion, the attempts to keep the faithful in ignorance by the clergy. But in the course of their studies, they cannot have failed to see the fact that in many areas of human life the Churches, through their teachings and through their actions, have brought forth positive fruits. Religiously inspired men advanced science and art; they worked, regardless of self, for the poorest sections of the population; they ventured into unknown parts not only in order to give the backward peoples that lived there their own faith, but also to make available to them the achievements of civilization. Religious conviction and a genuine, pure belief in God contributed a great deal to a realization of greater social justice; religious inspiration brought men incalculable cultural benefits. But the representatives of Eastern atheism and Eastern criticism of religion simply refuse to acknowledge these facts. Since they hold to a radically materialistic philosophy, religion can have no positive value for them.

The Tactics of Debate

It is clear that a debate with Eastern atheism cannot be limited to a rejection of the points of one's opponents, an account of the positive contributions of religion in the past and the present, but must also extend to the critical investigation of the philosophical basis of the Eastern criticism of religion. Eastern atheism and criticism of religion are based on the philosophy of dialectical and historical materialism. This philosophy starts from quite different assumptions from religious views. In any genuine discussion with representatives of Eastern atheism, this fact must never be overlooked. It has hardly any meaning to seek to prove to an Eastern atheist the truth of religion by means of the traditional proofs of God. For example, dialectical and historical materialism has no concept of the beginning of motion; thus, it cannot be refuted by the kinetic proof of God, which is based on the beginning of motion, and hence concludes that there must be a "prime mover". Dialectical and historical materialism knows no levels of being; thus, it is of little value to approach him with the proof of God that is based on the existence of levels of being. Dialectical and historical materialism does not have any concept of teleology, neither in animate nor inanimate nature, and so it would not be very open to the teleological proof of God.

Immanent Criticism of the Atheistic, Materialistic System

One can try, however, to move onto the plane of dialectical and historical materialism and, from this plane, show the inner contradiction, the self-contradiction of Eastern atheism. According to the idea of dialectical materialism, the universe represents a non-contingent reality that exists eternally and has always been involved in an evolution without beginning. "Evolution" is what the dialectical materialists call the movement that leads from the lower to the higher, from the simple to the more complex. If the universe, which today is at a certain level of evolution, was always involved in an evolution without beginning, then it would always have had to be at the present stage of its development, for where there is no beginning, there can be no development. But we can see a clear continuous evolution of the universe (e.g., the development of human society and culture, which is one feature of the universe). Thus, the human mind is forced to choose between two alternatives: either evolution has originated in time and, therefore, has only now reached the stage of present-day development and not already some higher one, or else the evolution of the universe had no beginning, since it is involved in an eternally rising and falling movement. In graphic terms, the first and only possible mode of development has the form of a line that runs from bottom to top; the second possibility, which would not be evolution, but only an eternal return of all things and phenomena, would be represented by a wavy line that has no absolute "up" and "down", but only an eternal swinging, without beginning and without end within a particular range.

In the former case, one is compelled to assume as absolute the beginning of the evolution of the universe, and in this acceptance there is also the idea of a transcendental principle that has determined and caused the moment of the entry of the universe into the evolutionary process. In the latter, the whole apparent "evolution" of the universe would be completely meaningless.

The logical conclusion of dialectical materialism would thus be to give up its atheistic character as incompatible with its conception of an evolution of the universe and of human history, or else to admit that cosmic evolution and human history is completely meaningless. But this admission would again contradict the nature of the Marxist-Leninist interpretation of history: historical materialism. Historical materialism regards human society as a reality that is in a state of development and as having a real history, and it sees history as a continuing process, the course of which does not consist in an eternal return of what once existed, but is a constant progression.

Conclusion

So much, then, for the attempt at a critical contribution to the problem of Eastern atheism. For the religious man, Eastern atheism is a test of his faith, perhaps the greatest one of history. He can break down because of it, if he fails to draw from the fact of the existence of such a great and active movement any lessons for his own attitude. But he can grow equally well as a result of it and deepen his faith by drawing the necessary conclusions, admitting his own shortcomings, doing something about them, and thus giving the world the example of a genuine, lived religious faith with which he will remove the basis from the East's criticism of religion.

PART III
DO-C DOCUMENTATION
CONCILIUM

Office of the Executive Secretary
Nijmegen, Netherlands

Phillip E. Berryman/*Panama City, Panama*

Infant Baptism in
Urban Latin America

I t is Sunday afternoon in a large Latin American city. People are ascending the church steps to present children for baptism. The parents stay home to prepare the fiesta while the godparents bring the children. Many have not been in the church since Holy Week or since their last baptism or funeral. Some visit the church for a devotion to a favorite saint. They call it a *templo* and, indeed, it is considered a kind of shrine to which they go for special prayers in time of need, for a Mass for a departed relative or a baptism. The priest's role is functional: he performs the rite for the customary amount of money.

The priest, on his part, tries to inject meaning into the ceremony which is now in the vernacular. But he feels frustrated with the knowledge that his explanations are not understood or appreciated. Earlier in the Sunday Masses he faced congregations which totaled several hundred people, almost all women and children, although there are 20,000 people in the parish. (The Latin American bishops have estimated Sunday observance at 3.5% of men and 9.5% of women[1] but among the poor in some sections it can be much lower yet.) Some of these children will receive instruction for their first communion, which may well

[1] F. Houtart and E. Pin, *The Church and the Latin American Revolution* (New York, 1965), p. 166.

159

be their last. People's religious awareness is a mixture of catechism concepts and popular ideas about God, heaven, hell, saints, sin, etc.

If we ask: "Where is the Church?", one answer could be "Everywhere." The great majority are baptized and consider themselves Catholic; church steeples punctuate the city and countryside; living rooms are decorated with Sacred Hearts, Virgins, and Last Suppers. Catholicism is integral to the people's lives, history and culture. But if we ask: "Where is the community which so lives in the spirit of Christ that it is a 'visible sacrament of saving unity'?" (*Constitution on the Church,* n. 9) the answer will be: "Almost nowhere." It is precisely this "everywhere/almost nowhere" presence of the Church which constitutes the crisis of Latin American Catholicism. If baptism is the entrance into the Church, what is the meaning of a baptismal ceremony that does not result in an adult decision to live as a member of this sacramental People of God? It is our contention that many baptisms do not arrive at their true significance and that our practice of immediately baptizing all infants presented must be re-examined.

In some contexts, immediate baptism of all infants presented is undoubtedly meaningful. Where the culture is deeply Christian and religious practice high, the presumption is that the infant will arrive at an adult life of faith. In pluralistic cultures, on the other hand, where church membership is a free option, the infant's family has made a free decision and he himself will later be confronted with the decision of faith. But in cultures where Catholicism is universal but largely nominal, many will never face the decision of faith, but will rather consider the Church a simple "fact of life".

Why are these people here for baptism? Several motives will appear in conversation. They wish to make the child Christian (from a Moor to a Christian!), to purify him from original sin, to put him in the grace of God. Above all, they have a vague but compelling notion about his fate if he dies without baptism. These phrases are echoes of the catechism and certainly part of

traditional belief. Quite common is the belief that baptism furnishes protection against illness. At a very deep level there is a
feeling that baptism is necessary to give a person his identity.
One young man, when asked why he wanted his daughter baptized, reflected a moment. "If you're not baptized, you're *nothing*," he answered. Most people seem to regard their baptismal
certificates as more important than their birth certificate. They
confer more status. The very fact that the stress is on the *padrinos*
and the fiesta—the parents often stay home—indicates that the
rite marks a significant event in the life of the family that is more
than religious. In short, the motives of the people have elements
of Christian dogma, magic and social significance. (We do not
wish to take to task the peoples of Latin America, for they are
not to blame for their lack of formation. It is simply that we
have personally experienced the anguish in Panama. In conversation with other priests from the Philippines, Congo, urban
Europe, etc., we have noted the same preoccupation.)

Recently, discussion of the question of infant baptism has appeared in print.[2] Generally these presentations have centered
around the relationships of sacraments and faith. We suggest
an aspect equally important, ecclesial community. Before stating
our analysis of the problematic, let us simply mention what we
consider to be presupposed as a theology of baptism. Our notion
of the meaning of infant baptism must be based on our understanding of adult baptism. In the New Testament Christian initi-

[2] P. Gerbe *et al.*, *Ils demandent le Baptême pour leur Enfant*: "Parole
et Mission" 10 (Paris-VIIe: Les Editions du Cerf, 1966), 256 pp. This
work contains a bibliography of articles in French publications during the
years 1962-1965. Also cf. recent articles in Paroisse et Liturgie: P. Van-
bergen and F. Compere, "L'Admission au Baptême des Nouveau-nés et
les Délais de la Célébration du Baptême," 2 (1966), pp. 98-113; A. Turck,
"Compte rendu d'une Enquête sur le Baptême des Enfants au Doyenné de
Saint-Denis," 2 (Paris, 1966), pp. 114-18; E. Marcus, "La Pastorale du
Baptême des Petits Enfants," 3 (1966), pp. 260-69; Equipe Sacerdotale
De Notre-Dame-Des-Champs, Paris, "Experience pour une Pastorale sur
la Foi et les Sacrements dans le Cadre du Baptême," 3 (1966), pp. 276-86;
"Le Baptême des Petits Enfants et les Recentes Decisions Pastorales de
l'Episcopat de France," 4 (1966), pp. 469-77. In Spanish we may note
F. Sebastian, "Sacramentos y Fe. Un Problema de la Pastoral Espanola,"
in *Iglesia Viva*, 2 (1966), pp. 75-85.

ation is a process: evangelization, faith, conversion, baptism, participation in the life of a Christian community. The crowds ask: "Brothers, what are we to do?" "Be converted and be baptized." Baptism is the embodiment of a man's conversion-decision. The whole process is conversion—but not simply conversion away from a certain way of life but rather to Christ in a community of believers. "And every day the Lord added to their number people who were saved" (Acts 2, 47).

We should note well that this community of believers is a definite group whose meetings and common life are inspired by the Gospel. Whatever else the New Testament writers say about baptism—that it is rebirth, death and resurrection, life in the spirit, life as a son, purification—it is always rooted in membership in the New People. In later theological terminology, we may say that the *sacramentum et res* of baptism is membership in the Church,[3] for its fundamental effect is a deputation to function as a member of the priestly people. In short, baptism is eminently ecclesial, for, on the one hand, it is creative of the Church (Eph. 5, 26ff.; Tit. 3, 5-7) and, on the other hand, it demands faith and conversion to conscious visible participation in the mission of the Church in the world.

With the foregoing presupposed, we pose the problematic of our present pastoral practice of infant baptism in Latin America as we see it.

1. *Conversion*

For the first Christians, baptism was the climax of a process that had begun with their first hearing of the Gospel, and it embodied their decision to enter the community of Christians. Today, we still see this process in adult baptisms. We may define Christian conversion as a decisive stand (sometimes but not necessarily occasioned by a crisis), by which one integrates and orients his whole life in Christ and commits himself as a member of the Church to his part in its mission. Must we not say that

[3] K. Rahner, *The Church and the Sacraments* (Quaestiones Disputatae, 9) (New York: Herder and Herder, 1963).

baptism, of its nature, demands an adult conversion? And if conversion is of the essence, does not honesty compel us to admit that in many cases our practice is a falsification of the sacrament?

2. *Faith*

Catholicism in Latin America is a cultural heritage which is practically universal, and hence, everyone is familiar with popular beliefs about God, the saints, heaven, hell, etc. But a truly adult, reflective, personal faith is relatively rare. Today it is common to speak of the distinction between "religion" and "Christian faith". "Religion", in this sense, is man's awareness of his relation to the Absolute, his sense of dependence and awe *vis-à-vis* superior forces. He seeks to relate himself to the Absolute by myth and ritual, especially in the so-called "rites of passage" that mark significant events: birth, adolescence, marriage, illness, death. "Christian faith", on the other hand is a personal commitment to Christ and acceptance of the Gospel of his death and resurrection and new life in his name. Religion is a natural need of man based on the human condition and the inescapable mystery of human life; faith is a free personal decision that is rooted in the concrete event of the incarnation and resurrection of Jesus of Nazareth and the Church begun in Jerusalem on Pentecost.

Religion is not totally opposed to faith. For a certain "faith" is a part of all genuine religion. And man's religious tendency is an opening for the Christian Gospel. But they are not identical. Many French pastors and theologians have the courage to say: "We know that in fact the majority of the people do not have, or no longer have, Christian faith." [4] And one French priest commenting on Brazil has said that the people have made up a natural religion and have called it the holy, Roman, Catholic and apostolic Church.

We do not wish to say here that the people of urban Latin America have lost their faith. On the contrary, traditional faith is

[4] Atelier Mission-Paroisses, "Pastorale Sacramentelle en Secteurs Dechristianises": Ch. 3 of *Ils Damendent* . . . , p. 68.

deep. Pastoral theologians of urban Europe divide the population into the "practicing", "non-practicing" and "non-believers", whereas in Latin America the great majority are "non-practicing" and there are few true "non-believers". But this faith has many elements of "natural religion". And it would seem that the natural need to observe significant events with "rites of passage" figures largely in the motivation for baptism (and indeed in other sacraments: first communion, matrimony, anointing, funeral Mass[5]). No one would claim that for most people in Latin America the conscious center of faith is the paschal mystery. Yet, baptism is a sacrament of faith.

3. *Membership*

What constitutes real membership in the Church? Canon law (CIC. 87) furnishes an easy answer: all the baptized in ecclesiastical communion who profess the Catholic faith. But if we reflect on the New Testament and ecclesiology, must we not see that real belonging demands coming together for the eucharist and working in common in the Church's mission? Do not people in urban Latin America simply accept the Church as a "fact of life" and not as a group identifiable in this world as the "Church"?

4. *Evangelization*

We turn from the parents who present children for baptism to those responsible for the pastoral practice of the Church. The Church's mission is not to sanctify the world by impersonal ritual action but to proclaim the Gospel to all men by all it does. But many people are baptized and never hear the Gospel. They receive a smattering of "Christian doctrine" but never hear the Good News that God is saving us and making us his people; the resurrection is perhaps a curiosity (even confused with reincar-

[5] We may mention that the problem here treated in reference to baptism affects the other sacraments. F. Sebastian, *art. cit.*, specifically treats of "baptisms without personal conversion", "confirmations without spiritual maturity", "eucharistic celebrations without fraternal community" and "marriages without the love of Christ for his Church".

nation) but not a central living truth. If our people are largely unevangelized, can we continue the present practice which simply perpetuates the condition? Must we not evangelize in connection with the celebration of baptism?

5. Sign-Community

The Church is to be a sign to the world. It must be a community of people visibly living in the spirit of Christ. And this sign-aspect should be seen in the sacramental celebrations of the community. But in a "Church" constituted simply by infant baptism, in a "Church" where there is no concrete community of faith, worship and brotherly service, in a "Church" whose practicing members are largely the old and pre-adolescents and which is practically devoid of men, is not the sign in danger of becoming a countersign?

The French Church has been preoccupied with this problem for some time. Hence, it comes as no surprise that the French episcopate has taken decisive action. After discussing it in Rome during the Council, early in 1966, they published a note on "The Pastoral Practice of Infant Baptism".[6] They begin by pointing out that many priests find themselves in a kind of "painful contradiction": they know that sacraments are meant to be sacraments of faith, yet, they often have the impression that people do not have sufficient faith. Since their viewpoint is pastoral, the bishops avoid theological issues on which there is no consensus (fate of unbaptized infants, nature of original sin and its effects, nature of sacramental causality), but declare what should be the pastoral stance toward families who present children for baptism. They relate baptism to the Church's salvific work by a double exigency: "(1) to bring every man salvation in Jesus Christ by baptism, sacrament of faith; (2) by the very life of the Church to give testimony of the call of Christ to all men."[7]

As a sign, baptism must clearly signify the true nature of the

[6] "La Pastorale du Baptême des Petits Enfants," in *Inf. Cath. Intern.* (1966), pp. 457-66.
[7] *Ibid.*, p. 460.

Church more than ever in today's world. The bishops stress heavily the *responsibility* for the children's *Christian education* as it affects *parents, pastors* and *Christian community*. The directives emphasize that there are two extremes to be avoided: excessive severity and excessive laxity; the former would presume to judge the faith of parents and immediately refuse or agree to baptize, while the latter would see no problem in immediate baptism of all infants presented and would thus practically ignore the fact that baptism of its nature must lead to real personal conversion, participation in the life of a Christian community and, above all, the eucharist. The bishops leave details to regional regulation, but they propose a catechumenate period for the parents (and possibly godparents) between a first "inscription" for baptism and the actual ceremony. This catechumenate means not only instruction but involvement in the life of the Church. They even envision the possibility of deferring baptism in some cases.

The French statement is admirable. But in connection with urban Latin America, one can see at least two differences in the situation. The French bishops seem to be stating a consensus: that there is a baptism problem and that a catechumenate for parents is essential. In Latin America there exists no such consensus in clergy or hierarchy. Furthermore, the French bishops seem to presuppose the existence of some ecclesial community to which the catechumenate could be related. In urban Latin America we submit that the Church is not present very often in ecclesial community, i.e., in a concrete group of people who know one another and act together as Christians. The minority of the population who attend Mass do not have the interrelationship of true community but are an aggregation of individuals drawn to the Church for motives of personal piety. (There is a real danger that because "community" is fashionable today, we will throw the word around and come to believe that it really exists.) To state it bluntly, while the French bishops speak of bringing non-practicing Catholics into a living experience of the

Church, in many milieux of Latin America there would be no place to go for such an experience.

We suggest that the baptism problem is simply a symptom of the deeper problem: that our people are not really evangelized and that the Church is not present as real ecclesial community. Hence, it would be illusory merely to institute some hasty baptismal instructions and proceed as before. Rather, the disparity between theology and reality in our practice should cause us to reflect on our whole pastoral work.

The solution would not be simply to refuse baptism to all except a small minority of model Christians or to establish some criterion such as marriage in the Church and Sunday Mass attendance. Catholicism is deeply rooted in the people. To seek to limit the Church at once would be to punish the poor and uninstructed for what is not their fault. We must rather offer them the opportunity of a *cheminement,* a growth toward maturity in the faith they profess.

The source of the pastoral problem is that baptism is considered a birthright, and Catholicism is part of everyone's cultural baggage. The *prime pastoral exigency* is then an *intelligent evolution* toward a state in which membership in the Church will be the result of a *free adult decision* and where the Church will act in society as *light and leaven.*

To mention one problem explicitly, the Church cannot be a Church of children and old women. In Latin America we must build up a Church of men and solid Christian married couples. But one of the greatest obstacles is the present piety and pastoral practice of saints and Marian devotions, an "other-worldly" attitude, and a spirituality of resignation and passivity. Each of these is a barrier to a man who lives by the challenge of the present and in a milieu that puts a high premium on masculinity. A true man cannot accept a "Christianity of escape". Perhaps the great majority of our men are correct in rejecting a Church too passive, too other-worldly, too identified with the status quo. The Church must involve men in the task to be done here and now, showing them the Christian meaning of their lives and engaging them in the struggle for unity, freedom and human dignity.

The priest must reflect on his image (sacrament-dispenser, officiant at funerals, assessor of pious societies, organizer of youth activities), and realize that his apostolate must be like that of the Lord himself: primarily dialogue with the men of his time about the exigencies of the Gospel. This means that he must put away whatever is a barrier to dialogue (e.g., the cassock, a system of support which depends on stole fees) and give prime time and importance to breaking out of routine to go out into the barrios. He must bring people together and enable them to discover the Church—to discover themselves as the Church. Through dialogue on their own lives and the fundamental themes of the Christian message in terms of their own experience, the priest and people can gradually build up a true local Christian community. In addition to this kind of evangelization we suggest the possibility of intense retreats or *cursillos* that could furnish the opportunity for real conversion decisions.[8]

The goal must be the formation of a truly evangelical community. But 20,000 people cannot be a community of people who know one another in the Lord. Christian community must be established on a more local level in the barrios with lay

[8] Here we are speaking from personal experience in Panama, chiefly in the parish of Cristo Redentor, San Miguelito, Panama City. The people of the parish are poor and largely immigrants from the interior of the country. In a short period of time (from March, 1963) a team of priests from Chicago, sisters and laymen have led in the formation of a truly marvelous Christian community. The "technique" (though it is far more *spirit* than technique) involves a course of formation called the "Family of God" and a Cursillo de Iniciacion Cristiana and a continuing program of formation and common life rooted both in the Gospel and real life. In passing we may note that this experience leads us to be rather optimistic about the possibilities of renewal in Latin America. If in this parish whole neighborhoods and sectors are being transformed by the movement of the parish, is it not possible that whole segments of our populations may be renewed by a form of Christianity that clearly champions the more truly human life our people yearn for? While some theologians and pastors are asserting almost dogmatically that the Church will be henceforth a minimal "remnant" of the general population, we suggest that in Latin America there is still the possibility of a Church of large numbers. But we must begin boldly with true local communities.

leadership, quite possibly, deacons. The large parish would be more of a communion of communities. These "cells" or "ecclesiolae", which meet in homes or apartments, should be concerned with concrete local problems as well as evangelization and liturgy celebration. The experience of intimate Christian community, which has seemed to be the privilege of "elite" apostolates, should be the normal experience of the Church. If the Church exists in such a form, it will be manifest that to be a Christian involves a definite, free commitment to others in Christ, made visible in a sacramental community, and that Christian life is not a resigned waiting period for the "other world" but an intense participation in the upbuilding of a more just and human order now.

Seen in relation to such a community, baptism can be given a more ecclesial sense: the entrance into this sacramental community and thereby into the universal Church. The ceremony could be reformed to make it clearly the baptism of a *child*, with appropriate parts for parents and godparents corresponding to their responsibilities. A communal ceremony would demonstrate that baptism is a first step, the *encaminamiento* on the journey of the pilgrim Church. The parents' preparation could be related to this type of ceremony.

It would seem that in Latin America we are generally not ready for norms like those given by the French episcopate because of our lack of consensus. An individual pastor who set up a program like that suggested in France (preliminary inscription of the child, group discussions, bible services, involvement in parish life, communal baptism ceremony) would probably find it self-defeating, for people would be able in most cases to find another parish that would baptize with no questions asked. Priests who seek to meet this problem will probably have to compromise with much more limited preparation of parents. But even more important is the renewal of the total apostolate.

In connection with this renewal we make some summary suggestions:

1. *Discussion:* We will not arrive at any effective action without dialogue and consensus on theological and pastoral issues. Sometimes differing theological conceptions of salvation, grace, Church, sacraments, etc., divide us. For example, there is a certain type of pastoral vision that is totally oriented (at least implicitly) toward bringing people to "die in the state of grace". The Council has provided a much wider perspective, e.g., the Church as the sacrament of God's unifying and saving action. We must honestly face up to the serious contradictions in our pastoral situation. Perhaps the statement of the French episcopate could serve as a starting point. Gradually we can come to our own consensus and common policy in the face of the exigencies of the Latin American pastoral situation.

2. *The Fee Question:* There is no doubt that to the majority of our people baptism is a "business" of the priest and not a celebration of the People of God. As difficult as it may be, we must begin to evolve out of a system that makes us dependent on stole fees, for this system is a stumbling block to the Gospel.

3. *Evangelization and Local Community:* We must initiate programs of dialogue and evangelization in the homes and apartments of the barrios. We are all surrounded by thousands of baptized people who have never heard the Gospel. Furthermore, our large parishes cannot provide the setting for the truly personal and communitarian Christianity demanded by our times. A baptism can be the occasion for the initiation of the parents and godparents into this movement.[9]

4. *Baptism Catechumenate:* There should be instituted an "inscription" of the child, a definite period before the actual baptism

---

[9] Reading the French literature on this question one gets the impression that there is no formal and organized program of evangelization of the general populace. It would seem that de-christianization has proceeded so far that one cannot call people together on the basis of their Catholic loyalty. However, in Latin America this is not true. It is still possible— and we would say essential—to make direct evangelization of the general population the principal apostolate.

(e.g., one month) in order to provide time for reflection and preparation. During this period the people can be invited to dialogue sessions on family life, the relation of Christian faith to real life, the parental responsibility for Christian formation of children, the meaning of baptism, etc. They should be given a chance to experience Christian community among some of the committed families of the parish. Even if they do not commit themselves at once to the movement of the parish, they should come away with more respect for what true Christianity is. One effect should be the clarification of motives for baptism. There should be fewer people seeking baptism as protection against illness or from purely social motives. If an eventual effect is a diminution in the number and percentage of the baptized, it will be simply a negative aspect of our evolution toward a mature Christianity.

Perhaps these paragraphs have seemed to wander far afield from the problematic of infant baptism. Nevertheless, we insist that this is precisely the type of reflection that our awareness of the disparity between theology and our present pastoral practice should lead to. The solution to the baptism problem in urban Latin America can be found only in confronting the wider pastoral exigency: the formation of genuine evangelical community.

Charlotte Hörgl / *Munich, West Germany*

Christian and Marxist Humanity

This year as in former years, the Paulusgesellschaft (which is concerned with the relations between the natural sciences, philosophy and theology) held its May meeting. From April 28 to May 1, 1966 on the Island of Herrenchiemsee in Bavaria, it continued discussing the subject of the previous year's meeting in Salzburg: Christian Humanity and Marxist Humanism.

At least 300 scholars and (chiefly journalistic) observers managed to find their way to this remote little island, demonstrating once again the steadily growing appeal of the Paulusgesellschaft and its concerns. Of course quantity did not exactly serve quality or make the exchange of opinions an easy matter. But the large number of participants at least gave expression to the large variety of opinions. These were in three groups. "Pure" (not always methodologically pure) science and neither for nor against either of the opposing ideologies of Marxism and Christianity. The natural sciences were principally represented by the Heidelberg physiologist, Professor Hans Schäfer.

The Marxist representation was much more disparate, committed either politically or scientifically, working in democratic freedom or under a dictatorial system. There were Communists from Eastern Europe (Hungary: Professor Joszef Szigeti, Budapest; Dr. J. Lukacs, Budapest; Czechoslovakia: Professor Erika

Kadlecova, Prague; Professor Miran Prucha, Prague; Professor J. Hromanka, Prague; Bulgaria: Professor A. Polikarov, Sofia; Roumania: Professor J. Gulian, Bucharest), from more moderate Yugoslavia (Professor V. Paviceivic, Belgrade; Professor O. Mandic, Zagrab; Professor B. Bosnjak, Zagreb) and from the West (Austria: Professor W. Hollitscher, Vienna; Italy: Professor Cesare Luporini, Florence; Professor A. Natta, Rome; Professor Lucio Lombardo-Radice, Rome; France: Roger Garaudy, Paris). The representatives from Moscow and East Germany were not allowed to come, nor was the chief representative from Poland, Professor Adam Schaf, Warsaw, who, one-and-a-half months before had been allowed to speak at the German opening of this series of Paulusgesellschaft talks. Unfortunately, the same can happen in non-Communist countries, for a Catholic theologian from Spain was forbidden to come.

The Christian representation was also international: Professor Prucha from Prague who admits to being a Christian as well as a Communist; the well-known Professor M. Dubarle from Paris, Professor Jules Girardi from Rome and Professor Gustav Wetter, Rome and Munich; the Spaniards: Professor Jesus Aguirre, Madrid, and Professor M. Siguan, Barcelona. Also present were Professor Helmut Thielicke, Hamburg, the speaker for the evangelicals, and for the Catholics, Professor Karl Rahner, Munich, and Professor Johannes B. Metz, Münster.

The scientists began according to the customs of the society. But they found themselves departing from the mainstream of the discussion, first, because they were not free enough from presuppositions (in his talk, Professor Schäfer slipped into philosophy); secondly, because the self-imposed methodological limitations of "pure" science require the absence of ideology, which naturally excludes pure scientists from an ideological debate. They were, therefore, unable to fill the role of a neutral bridge between the two other parties, as was originally planned.

Professor Schäfer made these points: in natural science man is distinguished from the animals; his definition is, therefore, a negative one. But the distinction must be made very delicately in all areas, not only the emotional and intellectual but also the morally analogous. But the natural sciences are still experimenting upon whether there are intelligent forms of behavior that "belong only to man". The superior development of man lies not so much in his "constantly overrated" power of reflection, as in his unconscious feedback of intelligent reflection. "The processes that chiefly determine men are, without any doubt, social feedbacks", which show themselves historically and are responsible for the ideas of various scientists about man and his possibilities, that is, for anthropology. At this point, he went beyond the scientific and spoke of religions and Christianity. Their notions, he said, cannot be scientifically established, but must be historically analyzed and then they would present anthropological implications, for "theology is extrapolated anthropology".

The discussion of his paper was not so much about the future possibilities of mankind arising out of the feedback theories, as about particular characteristics of man, such as his conscience and religious potentialities. But the contribution of the scientists was neither "pure" enough, nor widely enough based for the debate to be conducted at a fruitful level. There remained the ideologists, and they had brought with them all their presuppositions, even though they were prepared to express them moderately.

The optimism of the Marxist block at the first Salzburg Conference turned out to have been too hasty. Scholars from Marxist States had spoken euphemistically and cheerfully about the position of people and Christians in the East. But this year it became clear that they were still tied to the system, particularly in philosophical studies. As in the previous year, the Marxists from the West appeared to be ready and able to make greater concessions, as was seen particularly in the eloquent address of Professor Roger Garaudy from Paris. But it was not clear either from his talk or from the Italian representative, Professor Cesare Luporini from Florence, who was very ready for discussion, whether this was not just a rhetorically conciliatory tone or an *aggiornamento* arising simply out of their situation.

In the previous year the future had already been taken as the basis for common discussion, and although this time it was forced under the title "humanism", discussion of the "future", Christian and Marxist, seemed to be the means of a fruitful encounter. Moreover, the unhappy contrast between "Christian humanity" and "Marxist humanism" had already caused enough terminological difficulties and confusions to make everyone glad to turn to talking about the "future".

Of course, the Marxist talk of the future was primarily concerned with the proclamation of their essentially this-worldly and party-political goals. Only secondly did they admit Christianity as an existing means of conducting man in society toward the classless future. In all goodwill, Christianity was subjected as a means to an end. Luporini said that dialogue was now an historical necessity, for Marx's demand for an "atheist society" was no longer seen as necessary for the achievement of Marxist ends. The ethical and moral positions of *both* ideologies could lead to the desired "society without exploitation". Coexistence, an accident of politics made necessary by atomic research and technology, was thus with hindsight philosophically justified.

The more general opening remarks of the president of the Paulusgesellschaft, Professor Arthur Jores, Hamburg, were not in utopian accord with these conciliatory propositions. He said that in order for the cardboard-and-paper world of the ideologists to become a reality, not just the further humanization of mankind would be needed, but the ideologies themselves would have to get beyond their narcissistic ruminations over their own nature, and make up their minds really to serve their fellowmen and humanity. Even in the most open conversation, no cracks appeared in their rigid pictures of the world and of man. Coexistence appeared to be accepted or advocated as a platonic idea and because it was for the moment unavoidable.

Professor Garaudy admitted in a conciliatory way that since Christianity was the historical foundation of the whole of Western thought and philosophy, it was also literally fundamental to Marxism. He even amiably agreed that Marxism would be impoverished, if Christianity did not (any longer?) exist. But personal confessions of this nature made it plain that his open-minded attitude is only possible under a non-totalitarian system, and if there was a change of government, its advocates might suffer grievously.

The climax of Garaudy's paper was his dictum that the Marxists must become more Marxist and the Christians more Christian, and thence would arise a true "dialogue of hope". He was clearly demanding not so much an intellectual purification as, on both sides, a "pure" and dedicated service of man. But the purification of their teaching would sharpen their differences; this would hardly help the "dialogue". Their differences of opinion should show each other up, and then theory could turn again to practice.

The fundamental criticism of Marxism, as it appears in Garaudy's paper, is that it speaks of "man" but does not mean thereby particular men, but the human race, human society (even though particular people actually may "make their own lives"). This false humanism is also to be found in Christianity, in its past, present and hopes of the future, but for different reasons and purposes. On this occasion, well-meaning Christians, Metz in particular, might think that this overriding of the individual man is the only way to find a common ground on which to talk with the Marxists and to afford a real future to Christianity in the age of the organization man.

Metz spoke of the paradoxical modernity of the two-thousand-year-old biblical eschatology, the "operative future" as opposed to *contemplative* imprisonment in a subjective and metaphysical introversion. "The modern orientation toward the future and its implied understanding of the world as an historical process are founded upon the biblical promises" (Exod. 3, 14; Eph. 2, 22; 1 Thess. 4, 13). But because the true believer who really puts his trust in God does not know what the future will bring—unlike the this-worldly Marxist humanist who knows and surveys everything—it is proper for the future to work for the next thing coming and for one's neighbor, to "be for others" (Bonhoeffer). Just as our relationship to the "never-before-realized actuality of the future" is no longer one of pure contemplation and imagination, but on the contrary is highly operative; just as nature is no longer unapproachable and numinous, and is now rather the "scene of human historical action", so also it is not the *vestigia Dei* that are immediately evident in the world, but the *vestigia hominis,* his world-transforming actions and his reaching out into a future which he himself is perpetually creating. "What most mightily moves the modern man is not commitment to the other-worldly, but commitment to the future."

An understanding of the world thus orientated toward the future leads the Christian away from metaphysics and transcendence (which used to be the only foundations of their thought) toward a less magical-religious "humanism of creative hope". The master subject should not be theoretical philosophy, but politics which seeks and demands universal well-being, peace and justice for society, for every society in the world. For Metz this "political theology" is closely parallel to Marxist doctrines on society, on the whole of mankind which bears within it the promise of the final consummation, but only when we now fulfill this promise by our own deeds.

Luporini, in particular, took up Metz's point that he, too, saw the individual as contained by society, but in the discussion which followed, it became clear that Metz, unlike the Marxists, did not leave out of account the personal work and belief of the individual man. Transcendence, the future and personal commitment *together* constituted the biblical concept of man; and by society he meant a structured community of individual men with rights and duties.

This swift exposition and the interpretation of Metz's paper were supported by the remarks of Karl Rahner. The previous year, Rahner had already introduced the slogan "absolute future" into the talks, and this year stressed its importance, which went beyond our individual humanistic attitudes into the political and social order. In order not to overemphasize this aspect, he spoke with equal emphasis of the proper appreciation of the value of the person—more or less in open disagreement with the Marxists. Christian humanism was "concrete humanism" and was concerned with the individual and did not override him.

Unlike pre-Christian and non-Christian religions and modern ideologies, Christianity recognizes "the absolute importance and value of the concrete human person", who, therefore, may not "escape into the nothingness of time which will come to an end, and him with it". But the recognition of his absolute value must in practice be relative, for it implies respect and love for his fellowmen and is existentially limited by the human situation (i.e. above all, by the thought of death). His necessary "self-questioning" must be sublimated into an ever active love of his neighbor and into work for the world and society. The more truly human he is, the more he is prepared to lay his own absolute value aside and determine to help others.

Anthropology with its empirical and scientific method, necessary pluralism (for it is concerned with the whole range from natural sciences to philosophy) and Christian revelation had many and various things to say about man and the meaning and purpose of his life. But in spite of all this data, all we knew about him is that "he is the being that loses himself in God". Of course this is more a question of a theological statement, but it could say this for itself (Rahner continued): "Must we not say that we know what we know about man, from human sources and not from God, for we only know about God from human sources? Is theology, then, any more than *anthropologia negativa,* that is, the experience that man constantly disappears into the mystery that he can neither understand nor explain? And even when we realize that this *anthropologia negativa* does not make God a function or cipher of man, but places man before the *existing* absolute mystery, not created by him but making him know his own mortality, how is this a help to humanism?"

Although he must thus stand before the mystery and see death coming, which will also be the death of his humanism, this is no excuse for him to abandon the concrete humanism of the future. What he does and what he suffers both affect the future, the future that is hopeful and opaque. The particular vocation of the Christian is to personal, responsible action, and God's absolute future belongs to the *person* not to society or a particular society, and this personalization is implied in the trend of politics and the theology of pluralism.

With these remarks, Rahner summarized for the meeting and for the present stage of Christian thought the last possible word about humanism, at least as far as it can at present be expressed.

Thielicke, who followed him, did not maintain the scholarly tenor of the discussion and broke out into exaggerated and vulgar polemics. From his two-hour defense of Rahner, we can note his point that we must understand man as related to other men, toward whom man, understood in the personal sense, is always orientated.

The actual, if not terminological, agreement of the various positions led one to hope for future possible meetings of the Paulusgesellschaft. These would have more chance of success if the subject were properly defined and if they did not have to limit themselves to formal expositions that were not strictly representative. Due to the overcrowding at Herrenchiemsee some would-be contributors necessarily went unrepresented.

BIOGRAPHICAL NOTES

KARL RAHNER, S.J.: Born March 5, 1904, in Freiburg-im-Breisgau, Germany, he became a Jesuit in 1922 and was ordained in 1932. He earned his doctorate in theology in 1936. He has been professor of dogmatic theology at the University of Innsbruck, and professor of the philosophy of religion and of Christian anthropology at the University of Munich. In April, 1967, he will become professor of dogmatic theology and of the history of dogma at the University of Münster. After numerous theological writings (many of them translated into English) in which is expressed his central idea of an anthropocentric conception of the whole of theology, Rahner has come to be recognized as one of the most important theological thinkers of the German-speaking world.

CHARLES MOELLER: Born January 18, 1912, in Brussels, he was ordained in 1937. He pursued his studies at the University of Louvain and earned his doctorate in theology in 1941. He has taught at Louvain, and is presently Assistant Secretary of the Congregation for the Doctrine of the Faith. He played an important role in the preparation of the *Constitution on the Church* and the *Pastoral Constitution on the Church in the Modern World* of Vatican Council II. He is one of the founders of the Ecumenical Institute of Theological Research in Jerusalem, and a frequent contributor to reviews such as *Irénikon, Revue Nouvelle, Criterio* and *Revue d'Histoire Eccl.* Among his published works is *L'homme moderne devant le salut* (Paris, 1965).

THEODORE STEEMAN, O.F.M.: Born April 13, 1928, in Rotterdam, he became a Franciscan and was ordained in 1953. He pursued his studies at the Universities of Leiden and Harvard, and is presently preparing his doctoral thesis. He is a member of the Board of Directors of the Catholic Institute of Social and Religious Research (K.A.S.K.I., The Hague). Among his published works is *The Study of Atheism: A Sociological Approach* (Louvain, 1965). He is a contributor to *Social Compass.*

JULES GIRARDI, S.D.B.: Born February 23, 1926, in Cairo, he became a Salesian of Don Bosco and was ordained in 1955. He pursued his studies at the Pontifical Salesian University in Turin and at the Gregorian University in Rome. He earned his doctorate in philosophy in 1950, and is presently professor of metaphysics and the history of contemporary philosophy at the Pontifical Salesian University. He is also chairman of the editorial committee of the encyclopedia *L'Athéisme contemporain.* Among his published works is *Theologia naturalis* (1962). He contributes to the *Revue Philosophique de Louvain.*

KARL LEHMANN: Born May 16, 1936, in Freiburg-im-Breisgau, he was ordained in 1963. He studied at the Universities of Freiburg-im-Breisgau and Munich, as well as at Gregorian University in Rome. He earned his doctorate in philosophy in 1962 and his degree in theology in 1964. He is presently an assistant to Karl Rahner at the University of Munich. He is a contributor to *Lexikon für Theologie und Kirche* and to *Handbuch der Pastoraltheologie*.

JACQUES LOEW: Born August 31, 1908, in Clermont-Ferrand, France, he was ordained in 1939. He is Superior of the Mission Ouvrière Saints Pierre et Paul, and also a consultant to the Secretariat for Non-Believers. Among his published works is the seven-volume *Foi vivante, hommes d'aujourd'hui* (Editions du Cerf).

PAUL MATUSSEK: Born February 1, 1919, in Berlin, he pursued his studies at the Universities of Berlin and of Heidelberg. He earned his doctorate in philosophy in 1944 and his doctorate in medicine in 1946. He is presently professor of neurology and psychiatry at the University of Munich. Among his published works is *Ideologie, Glaube und Gewissen*, with Richard Egenter (1965). He contributes regularly to *Confinia Psychiatria*.

VINCENZO MIANO, S.D.B.: Born June 28, 1910, in Canicattini, Italy, he became a Salesian of Don Bosco and was ordained in 1934. He pursued his studies at the University of Pisa and at the Gregorian University in Rome, earning his doctorate in theology in 1941. He has taught fundamental theology and philosophy and is presently Secretary to the Secretariat for Non-Believers. Among his published works is *Problemi di Gnoseologia e Metafisica*. He contributes regularly to *Divus Thomas* and to *Salesianum*.

ERWIN ADLER: Born October 9, 1934, in Hindenburg, Germany, he pursued his studies at the Universities of Innsbruck, Münster and Munich, and earned his doctorate in philosophy in 1962. He is the author of various publications on Marxism, and he contributes to the review *Sowjet-Studien* (Munich).

PHILLIP E. BERRYMAN: Born March 22, 1938, in Los Angeles, he was ordained in 1963. He studied at St. John's Seminary in Camarillo, California, and was a member of the experimental Cristo Redentor team in San Miguelito, Panama. He works with the Pastoral Institute in Panama, where he presently has a parish.

CHARLOTTE HÖRGL: Born January 10, 1935, in Munich, she studied at the University of Munich, where she graduated in theology. She earned her doctorate in philosophy in 1962, and presently lectures at the University of Munich. Among her writings is, "Die göttliche Erziehung des Menschen nach Irenäus," in *Oikumene: Studien zum Vaticanum II* (1964).

International Publishers of CONCILIUM

ENGLISH EDITION
Paulist Press
Glen Rock, N. J., U.S.A.

Burns & Oates Ltd.
25 Ashley Place
London, S.W.1

DUTCH EDITION
Uitgeverij Paul Brand, N. V.
Hilversum, Netherlands

FRENCH EDITION
Maison Mame
Tours/Paris, France

GERMAN EDITION
Verlagsanstalt Benziger & Co., A.G.
Einsiedeln, Switzerland

Matthias Grunewald-Verlag
Mainz, W. Germany

SPANISH EDITION
Ediciones Guadarrama
Madrid, Spain

PORTUGUESE EDITION
Livraria Morais Editora, Ltda.
Lisbon, Portugal

ITALIAN EDITION
Editrice Queriniana
Brescia, Italy